Strange

Ohio

Monsters

Michael Newton

Schiffer
Publishing Ltd

4880 Lower Valley Road • Atglen, PA 19310

Schiffer Books are available at special discounts for bulk purchases for sales promotions or premiums. Special editions, including personalized covers, corporate imprints, and excerpts can be created in large quantities for special needs. For more information contact the publisher:

Published by Schiffer Publishing, Ltd.
4880 Lower Valley Road
Atglen, PA 19310
Phone: (610) 593-1777; Fax: (610) 593-2002
E-mail: Info@schifferbooks.com

For the largest selection of fine reference books on this and related subjects, please visit our website at **www.schifferbooks.com.**

We are always looking for people to write

books on new and related subjects. If you have an idea for a book, please contact us at proposals@schifferbooks.com.

This book may be purchased from the publisher.
Please try your bookstore first.
You may write for a free catalog.

Designed by RoS
Type set in Domingo/Book Antiqua

ISBN: 978-0-7643-4397-1
Printed in China

Other Schiffer Books By The Author:

Strange Kentucky Monsters
ISBN: 978-0-7643-3440-5 $14.99

Strange California Monsters
ISBN: 978-0-7643-3336-1 $14.99

Strange Indiana Monsters
ISBN: 0-7643-2608-2 $12.95

Strange Monsters of the Pacific Northwest
ISBN: 978-0-7643-3622-5 $16.99

Strange Pennsylvania Monsters
ISBN: 978-0-7643-3985-1 $19.99

Birmingham, Alabama: Ku Klux Terror
ISBN: 978-0-7643-4364-3 $16.99

text and images by author unless otherwise noted

Dedication

For Jim and Mary Alice,
rescuing all creatures, great and small.

DOGMAN

...and he's not happy

BRALER PRODUCTIONS, INC AND DOGMAN FILM ASSOCIATES, LLC
PRESENT
LARRY JOE CAMPBELL · MARIAN MAVERRY
KIMBERLY NORRIS GUERRERO · STACIE HADGIKOSTI
TOM CILLUFFO · LUKE BONCZYK
ASSOCIATE PRODUCER KIM ECKSTEIN · MUSIC BY GRANT FLOERING
EDITED BY RUPERT TOMLINSON
Written and Directed by RICH BRALIER

CREATURE
FROM THE
BLACK LAGOON

RICHARD CARLSON · JULIA ADAMS
RICHARD DENNING · ANTONIO MORENO · NESTOR PAIVA · WHIT BISSELL

The Legend of
GRASSMAN

Contents

Monstrous

Ohio

Ohio takes its name from an Iroquois word meaning "great river." Originally part of America's vast Northwest Territory, incorporated in 1787, it became the Union's seventeenth state in 1803. Today, it is the country's 34th largest state in area, ranked as the seventh most populous, and the tenth most densely populated, with 282 residents per square mile.[1] However, as we've seen in other installments of the Strange Monsters series, such official statistics may not be strictly accurate.

For starters, 2,108,636 of Ohio's citizens (18.2 percent) live in just 6 of the state's 251 cities: Akron, Cincinnati, Cleveland, Columbus, Dayton, and Toledo. Furthermore, 3,890 of the state's 44,825 square miles (8.7 percent) are under water, submerged beneath Ohio's 50,000 lakes and ponds, some 2,600 of which drown two acres or more. Nor are we finished yet. Another 14 percent of the state's total area — 6,293 square miles in all — is held by the state or federal government as parks, forest, or nature preserves, and wildlife management areas.[2]

Seen from that perspective, Ohio's population density is actually 333 persons per square mile on inhabited turf, with much of that being urban. Meanwhile, wildlife thrives in the state's forests and marshes, in lakes, ponds, and rivers. Official spokesmen recognize 186 species of fish, 39 species of amphibians, 45 species of reptiles, 141 nesting species of birds, and 59 species of mammals living statewide.[3]

And once again we are compelled to ask: are those statistics accurate? Has anything been overlooked?

From the reports collected in this volume, it appears that much has been ignored, denied outright, or briefly noted in some dossier and then left unexplained. Unless the Buckeye State has far more than its share of drunkards, arrant liars, or delusional psychotics, there are creatures still unknown inhabiting Ohio's wilds, including some that mystify and frighten witnesses who meet them in the course of daily life.

Many of those elusive beasts may qualify as cryptids — "hidden" or "unexpected" animals pursued by students of cryptozoology. Such creatures fall into 4 broad categories:

1. Members of known species reported from areas where they should not exist in the wild
2. Animals resembling members of a known living species, but diverging greatly in size (giants or pygmies) and/or displaying variations in color or form unknown for their species
3. Apparent living members of species officially classified as extinct worldwide or extirpated from a given area
4. Creatures unrecognized by science as belonging to any known species of the past or present

Cryptozoology is not an occult field of study. It has nothing to do with ghosts, shape-shifters, magic, or the walking dead — but some of Ohio's odd inhabitants are said to behave in ways that defy known capabilities of any flesh-and-blood creature. I include them here, without endorsement, because "monsters," after all, may dwell as much in human minds as on the streets or in the woodlands of our 3-dimensional reality.

Strange Ohio Monsters is divided into 8 topical chapters, covering the full scope of unknown, uninvited creatures that have been reported from within the state.

Chapter 1 describes assorted animals misplaced in habitat or time, alien invaders, and species that refuse to disappear, although officially wiped out.

Chapter 2 surveys reports of surviving Ohio cougars, supposedly extirpated more than 100 years ago, yet still seen frequently, alive and well.

Chapter 3 reviews sightings of other mystery cats, apparent members of exotic species alien to the Midwest and North America at large.

Chapter 4 examines reports of outlandish reptiles, including snakes and lizards, dwarfing the largest species known on Earth.

Chapter 5 charts the appearance of aquatic cryptids in Ohio, commonly dubbed "lake monsters," reported from the dawn of local history.

Chapter 6 collects case histories of eerie things with wings, inhabiting Ohio's haunted skies.

Chapter 7 analyzes Buckeye reports of hairy giants, known elsewhere as Bigfoot or Sasquatch, apparent apes or primates unrecognized by science.

Chapter 8 completes the roundup with reports of creatures that defy classification, some strange enough to leave the mind reeling in shock.

The crypto safari starts now.

Chapter 1

Out of Place, Out of Time

O hio's 470 species of fish, amphibians, reptiles, birds, and mammals represent a healthy wildlife population for a state teeming with humans. Granted, some are suffering: the state's list of endangered species includes 23 fish, 5 amphibians, 5 reptiles, 16 birds, and 5 mammals.[1]

Cryptozoologists are more concerned with beasts that don't belong, invasive species out of place within the Buckeye State. Wildlife authorities acknowledge 12 species of "alien" crustaceans inhabiting Ohio waters, but our focus — as stated in 1982 by Dr. Bernard Heuvelmans, the "Father of Cryptozoology" — runs to creatures of appreciable size. With that in mind, Ohio recognizes 9 invasive species, 8 aquatic and 1 terrestrial.[2]

Something Fishy

All but one of the state's aquatic invaders are American natives, simply misplaced in Ohio. They include the American eel (*Anguilla rostrata*), black buffalo (*Ictiobus niger*), bluegill (*Lepomis macrochirus*), Mexican tetra

---

Piranhas and closely related pacus are reported in Ohio waters.
Credit: U.S. Fish & Wildlife Service

(*Astyanax mexicanus*), orangespotted sunfish (*Lepomis humilis*), redear sunfish (*L. microlophus*), pumpkinseed (*Lepomis gibbosus*), river carpsucker (*Carpiodes carpio*), warmouth (*Lepomis gulosus*), and white crappie (*Pomoxis annularis*). The ninth, and the only exotic species, is listed as an "unidentified pacu" from Latin America.[3]

This brings us to the sticky subject of invaders from the Amazon.

Pacus belong to the subfamily *Serrasalminae*, and are divided into 9 genera, each containing 1 or more species. They are related to piranhas, but are harmless to humans — and, in fact, are known among aquarium breeders as "vegetarian piranhas."[4] The problem arises when pacus, or something like them, are caught in Ohio waters.

More specifically, are anglers hooking pacus or piranhas?

Piranhas belong to the family *Characidae*, with 4 genera recognized by their specialized interlocking teeth. The subject of various Hollywood horror films — sometime incorrectly dubbed "cannibal fish" for allegedly devouring humans, whereas true cannibals eat their own species — piranhas are in fact omnivorous, rarely deserving their legendary reputation.[5] Still, the appearance of piranhas or their tropical relatives in chilly Ohio waters is both perplexing and potentially alarming.

A map posted online by state wildlife officials notes two undated encounters with pacu from Lake Erie, listing the species as "failed/extirpated/eradicated."[6] Media reports, often confused and contradictory, suggest more frequent appearances of tropical invaders, on a wider scale.

In early June 2007, for example, young angler Kyle Owens pulled "a piranha-like fish" from the Ohio River, at Chilo, in Clermont County. The owner of a local exotic fish store opined that his catch was "probably" a pacu, but no formal identification was made. Neither Cincinnati's zoo nor the Newport Aquarium would accept the specimen.[7]

Four years later, in August 2011, Michael Cline caught a pacu at Buckeye Lake, on the Fairfield-Licking County line. An officer from the Ohio Division of Wildlife confirmed the fish's identity, logically suggesting that it was dumped in the lake by a negligent owner.[8]

Less than a month elapsed before the next strange catch, at Brown County's Grant Lake, where fishermen Jake Sizemore and Larry Waits reportedly caught an 8-inch red-bellied piranha (*Pygocentrus nattereri*) in early September 2011. Waits recognized the species on sight, he said, since he had caught a nearly identical fish at the same lake in June 2010. The latter specimen was televised, one viewer declaring from a brief view of its teeth that it was, in fact, a pacu.[9]

Gator Bait

One of Ohio's premier historical sites is the nationally-recognized Alligator Effigy Mound at Granville, in Licking County. Presumably built by members of the Fort Ancient aboriginal culture sometime between 800 and 1200 C.E., when seen from the air, the mound resembles a sprawled quadruped with a long, curving tail. Its round head bears no likeness to that of an alligator—and some researchers claim it actually depicts a salamander, an opossum, or a mythic "underwater panther," but the alligator tag endures in directories published by the National Park Service.[10]

Prehistoric constructions aside, there should be no alligators or other crocodilians (order *Crocodilia*) in Ohio, outside of zoos or private collections. And yet, they still appear sporadically in the wild.

Alligators found at large in Ohio may be exotic pets released by negligent owners. *Credit: U.S. Fish & Wildlife Service*

The first such encounter dates from July 6, 1935, when a gator 3 feet long was caught at Xenia, in Greene County. The *New York Times* identified the site as "Huffman Pond," apparently referring to present-day Huffman Reservoir. British authors Colin and Janet Bord describe the reptile as a crocodile, misstating its date of capture as July 1936.[11]

Nearly 7 decades elapsed before the next crocodilian surfaced in Ohio, at Acron's Arlington Plaza, on January 29, 2003. It was a juvenile American alligator (*Alligator mississippiensis*), curiously caught inside the corporate office of Northcoast PCS, a mobile telephone company (now Revol Wireless). Manager George Garcia, an inveterate practical joker, admitted to planting the foot-long reptile on-site to alarm his employees.[12]

September 2004 brought reports of a "marsh monster" haunting Mentor Marsh, in Lake County. Officers from the Ohio Division of Natural Areas and Preserves captured the beast on September 23, proclaiming it a 3-foot-long caiman (subfamily *Caimaninae*) of indeterminate species.[13]

Another specimen turned up in Canton's Nimishillen Creek, near Malone College, on October 2, 2006. A firefighter caught the reptile bare-handed and delivered it to biology professor Chris Carmichael, who identified it as an American alligator.[14]

Teenage angler Robert Pendleton Jr. caught the first of several alligators pulled from Akron's Summit Lake on July 18, 2007. It measured 5 feet long and was delivered to the Humane Society of Akron pending permanent settlement elsewhere.[15]

In the predawn hours of July 23, 2008, police lieutenant Anthony Fish caught an alligator measuring 27 inches on Mill Street, in Athens, Ohio. He delivered it to the Hocking Woods Nature Center at Hocking College, where administrators opined that the reptile was abandoned by an unknown student at nearby Ohio University.[16]

Eastlake, in Lake County, witnessed the next crocodilian visitation in August 2008. Authorities tried their best to snare the rambling reptile, and a representative from the Cleveland Metroparks Zoo actually netted it in the Chagrin River, on September 10, but the 3-foot specimen tore its way free and fled to parts unknown.[17]

Roy Hatcher, from the Columbus Zoo and Aquarium, had an easier time with a 10-pound gator found at Grove City on November 24, 2008. Cold had sapped the reptile's strength, making it an easy catch.[18]

Akron eighth-grader Anthony Greer caught the Buckeye State's next crocodilian visitor at Summit Lake, on April 19, 2009. He claimed that the 48-inch reptile lunged at him while he was fishing, forcing him to kill it with a brick. A silver band on the gator's right-rear foot bore the number "483," prompting Akron Zoo manager Pete Mohan to speculate that it was "a poached animal, or stolen."[19]

Less than two months later, on July 9, residents of Newcomerstown reported a 4-foot alligator sunning itself beside the Tuscarawas River. Sheriff Walt Wilson investigated, learning that Police Chief Tim Miller had photographed the reptile 3 days earlier. No help was forthcoming, as the DNR denied jurisdiction over exotic species and Akron's zoo cited a law banning acceptance of stray gators.[20]

While that scaly visitor dodged all attempts at capture, another crocodilian turned up at the Riverside Athletic Club in Hamilton, on July 25, 2009. Police sergeant Craig Bucheit caught the gator, measuring 3 and a half feet long, on the bank of the Miami River, deeming its appearance "definitely unusual for around here."[21]

Jeff Tate, owner of Buckeye Caseworks in Columbus, arrived at work on June 17, 2010, to find a 4-foot gator loitering outside his place of business, in a mud puddle. Police arrived, then summoned Chris Law from Ohio Reptile Rescue, who captured the creature without incident.[22]

On June 28, 2010, Cleveland police logged a report of a 4-foot alligator roaming through Ridge Square Park. What they found on arrival was a two-foot-long caiman, easily captured, but no Ohio zoo would accept the reptile due to its unknown origin. Later that night, Wildlife Officer Hollie Fluharty executed the hapless beast with a gunshot to the head.[23]

Akron angler Adrian Diaz hooked Summit Lake's third alligator on July 7, 2010. As he was reeling in the 42-inch reptile, a larger specimen — 6 feet at least, by Diaz's estimate — surfaced nearby and made a menacing noise. Diaz fled with his catch, later delivered to animal wardens, while its presumed parent remained at liberty.[24]

Guernsey County sheriff's deputies found a 3-foot alligator sunning along Crooked Creek, near Cambridge, on May 12, 2011. Again, the DNR denied any legal authority to collect exotic species. Again, the reptile was shot.[25]

On September 13, 2011, a Columbus motorist reported an alligator ambling along Interstate 270. Officer Joshua Gantt responded and caught the small reptile alive, transporting it to Ohio Reptile Rescue for eventual resettlement in Florida. A short article posted online described the gator as the third caught by Columbus police so far in 2011.[26]

Just over two weeks later, On September 30, employees at a sewage treatment plant in Hamilton pulled an 11-inch alligator from malodorous water at their workplace. They delivered it to Arrowhead Reptile Rescue, where spokesman Damien Oxier surmised that some cruel owner had flushed it down a toilet.[27] The same explanation is sometimes offered in response to claims of gators inhabiting sewers in major American cities.

In each case cited here, authorities explained crocodilian captures or sightings with reference to deliberate release of exotic pets. In fact, the Buckeye State had no laws governing private ownership of alien species until early 2012, when public outcry over an incident detailed in Chapter 3 prompted passage of a statute banning importation of exotic species "unless an animal is in full compliance with all other state and federal agencies [*sic*] rules and regulations" and certified free of disease. Even now, no legal limitation is imposed specifically on wild animals potentially dangerous to humans.[28]

Meandering Monitors

The largest known lizards still living on Earth are the monitors (genus *Varanus*), including 96 recognized species and subspecies. Largest among them is the Komodo dragon (*Varanus komodoensis*) of Indonesia, unknown to science before 1910.[29]

The monitors are Old Word lizards, natives of Africa, Asia, and Oceania, but they have found their way to the Western Hemisphere by one means or another, and at least one species—the Nile monitor (*V. niloticus*)—has established breeding colonies in Florida.[30] Others have been found within Ohio.

The first Buckeye monitor met an untimely fate on February 22, 1984, when teenage hunter Rodney Cameron shot and killed it at a pond in his family's backyard in Findlay. Presumed to be an escaped or abandoned pet, the Nile monitor measured 5 feet, 11 inches long.[31]

More recently, on September 28, 2010, two separate witnesses reported a lizard 4 to 5 feet long prowling the streets of Janesville. Police searched in vain, surmising that the reptile had escaped into a sewer drain.[32]

Monitor lizards are available for sale in Ohio.
Credit: U.S. Fish & Wildlife Service

Perusal of newspaper classified ads or a quick search online reveals that various species of monitors are offered for sale in Ohio, along with other exotic reptiles. Wildlife authorities insist that no large alien reptiles can survive harsh Buckeye winters in the wild, but as we'll see in Chapter 4, some very large—and still unidentified—species seem to have done just that.

Hog Wild!

Feral swine (*Sus scrofa*) are the only exotic mammals acknowledged by Ohio's Department of Natural Resources, with breeding populations established in several locations spanning the southern half of the state. Native to Eurasia and North Africa, wild hogs were introduced to the continental United States in 1539 and presently inhabit at least 35 states.[33]

Adult feral swine commonly weigh 125 to 300 pounds, and while Ohio specimens rarely exceed 350 pounds, imposing giants have been shot in other states, including the 800-pound "Hogzilla" killed by Georgia hunters in 2004 and Alabama's "Pigzilla" slain 3 years later, allegedly weighing 1,051 pounds.[34]

Ohio breeding colonies of feral swine have been confirmed in Adams, Ashtabula, Athens, Belmont, Gallia, Hocking, Jackson, Lawrence, Monroe, Ross, Scioto, and Vinton counties, with occasional unverified sightings from other regions. Noting the damage caused to crops and other natural resources, in addition to 30 known viral diseases and 37 parasites, wildlife officers encourage "harvesting" of hogs wherever they are found.[35]

Such risks aside, large feral hogs may also pose a physical danger to humans, their livestock, and pets. Researcher Ron Schaffner reports one such case from December 2, 1989, when 4 hunters were rushed by 6 or 7 hogs weighing 300 to 400 pounds apiece, sporting two-inch tusks. The men killed 4 of the aggressive hogs at close range, while several others escaped.[36]

The Cavies Are Coming!

Ignored by state officials are two recent reports of large South American rodents at large in Ohio. The first account, confirmed by physical remains, comes from Amelia, in Clermont County. There, on September 11, 2003, residents found a "mystery animal" with a broken leg hobbling along a rural road. Transported to All Creatures Animal Hospital, it was identified as a Patagonian cavy or mara (*Dolichotis patagonum*), native to Argentina.

Dr. Linda Meakin at All Creatures told reporters, "It does not make a good pet. Somebody obviously had it as a pet, but I would not recommend that. I would stick with the usual cats and dogs." Plans were announced to put the cavy up for adoption if its presumed owner did not appear.[37]

Two years later, on September 22, 2005, Cindy Knisley of South Charleston called police to report a kangaroo blocking her driveway. The creature hopped away as she approached it, and Sheriff Gene Kelly dismissed the notion of Buckeye kangaroos—although, as we shall see in Chapter 8, they're not unheard of. Knisley described the beast as a quadruped, 3 feet tall, weighing about 30 pounds. After conducting an Internet search, she changed her initial I.D. and announced its resemblance to a Patagonian cavy. The furry fugitive was nearly cornered on September 23, then managed to escape from a posse armed with blankets and a tranquilizer gun.[38]

Dead and Gone?

Ohio wildlife officials maintain a list of native species extirpated since the state was settled by European immigrants. It includes 1 butterfly, 13 molluscs, 5 fish, 4 birds, and 9 mammals. A separate list of extinct native species—officially no longer living anywhere on Earth—includes 5 molluscs, 2 fish, and 2 birds.[39]

Three mammalian species from the extirpated list concern us here, based on continuing reports of their existence in the wild. One, the eastern cougar, has been seen so often since the news of its demise that it rates separate coverage in Chapter 2. The other apparent survivors are the porcupine (*Erethizon dorsatum*) and the timber wolf (*Canis lupus*).[40]

Porcupines rank as the second-largest North American rodent, after beavers. State spokesmen offer no date for the porcupine's eradication from Ohio, but they are adamant in listing it as extirpated. In January 2006, when a hiker photographed a porcupine at the Blue Heron Reserve northeast of Fremont, park officers confirmed the critter's identity but dismissed it as another discarded pet. According to Brian Bury, state wildlife officer assigned to the county, "Somebody probably picked it up in Michigan and brought it back as a pet and just got tired of it."[41]

Perhaps. But what, then, do we make of out next case? In January 2012, the *Columbus Dispatch* reported that a bobcat had been shot in Mahoning County. Its stomach contained porcupine quills and one of the hapless rodent's hind feet, "although where an Ohio bobcat found a porcupine remains unanswered."[42]

Ohio authorities declared a "war of extermination" against wolves in 1818, announcing, in 1842, that the state's last wild specimen had been slain.

Nonetheless, Sandusky County hunter Dusty Gore shot a wolf at Bellevue on March 19, 2010. While wildlife officers quickly dismissed it as an wayward pet, locals reported "as many as 7 packs of wolves" roaming the county.[43]

Three residents of Dover, in Tuscawaras County, reported wolf sightings on June 13 and 16, 2011. The county's dog warden set a trap for the creature, without result. Sightings spread to New Philadelphia in July, with officials judging the beast sight-unseen as a dog-wolf hybrid escaped from captivity. The case remains unproven, since the animal eluded its pursuers.[44]

Missing Lynx

Knowledgeable sources seem confused over the status of the Canada lynx (*Lynx canadensis*) in Ohio. Early settlers penned descriptions of the cats, sometimes calling them "panthers" or "wildcats," the latter term also applied to smaller but related bobcats (*Lynx rufus*). Today, thanks to over-

Ohio lynx sightings continue despite the cat's supposed 19th-century extirpation.
Credit: U.S. Fish & Wildlife Service

hunting and habitat destruction, Ohio's DNR lists them as extirpated from the state. While no specific date is cited for the death of the last Buckeye lynx, most sources agree that the cats were wiped out by the mid-nineteenth century. The U.S. Fish and Wildlife Service claims the lynx's present range includes 14 of the contiguous United States: Washington, Oregon, Idaho, Montana, Wyoming, Colorado, Utah, Minnesota, Wisconsin, Michigan, New York, Vermont, New Hampshire, and Maine. [45]

It came as a surprise, therefore, when Auglaize County farmer Albert Adams shot a lynx near Buckland on January 5, 1918. Before its demise, the cat had raided homesteads in the area, devouring geese and chickens. According to the *Lima Daily News*, the dead lynx measured 5-foot-2 inches in length and stood 27 inches tall at the shoulder. If true, the cat was significantly larger than most of its species, whose males average 33.5 inches long and boast a record length of 3-foot, 5 inches. Nor does the larger Eurasian lynx (*L. lynx*) measure up to the Buckland specimen, with a record length of 4 feet, 3 inches. [46]

Auglaize County residents recalled another lynx killed in their neighborhood, in 1892, and sightings continue from Ohio to the present day, with the latest on record reported from Westlake on December 12, 2011. [47] A possibility exists of witnesses mistaking bobcats for their larger cousins, and it may be argued that a stray lynx wanders south from Canada or rare occasions. Likewise, the exotic pet trade may explain some sightings. As this volume went to press, at least one Buckeye breeder, based in Bluffton (straddling the Allen-Hancock County line) offered lynx kittens for sale online at $1,800 per cat.

Bothered Over Bobcats

Similar confusion surrounds the history of bobcats in Ohio. While their cousins, the Canada lynx, are listed as an extirpated Buckeye species, bobcats occupy a place on the endangered list. Still, published reports state that bobcats "could no longer be found living in the state" after 1850. [48] Once again, however, that was not the end of the story.

A scattering of unverified sightings in the 1960s heralded the bobcat's return—if, in fact, the cats were ever gone at all. Between 1970 and 2008, wildlife officers verified 255 sightings from 31 counties, with most of the latter year's reports logged from Noble County and environs. Verification was confirmed from photographs, sightings by DNR agents, and incidental trappings where the cats were identified and released. Another 214 unverified sightings were also reported in 2008. [49]

Julie Morgan of Boston Heights, in Summit County, caught a bobcat on film with her backyard motion-activated camera on September 19, 2010. Lisa Petit, resource manager for nearby Cuyahoga Valley National Park, reported a 3-year series of unverified sightings prior to Petit's delivery of iron-clad proof.[50]

And sightings multiplied from there. Wildlife authorities acknowledged 106 verified sightings for 2010, up from 92 in the previous year. Those cases brought the state's total to 464 verified sightings in 33 counties since 1970, with the number growing steadily.[51]

...which begs the question: if Ohio's bobcats can rebound so dramatically from official nonexistence, what of the state's largest felid, allegedly wiped out 5 years before the "last" bobcat was killed?

Bobcats have made a dramatic comeback from near-extermination in Ohio. *Credit: U.S. Fish & Wildlife Service*

Chapter 2

The Cat Came Back

Penned by American composer Henry S. Miller in 1883, "The Cat Came Back" was a popular song depicting the efforts of one Mister Johnson to rid himself of an "old yaller cat" he despised. No matter what he tries, the cat returns until an organ grinder plays a certain tune, whereupon "de cat dropped dead."[1]

According to official records, Ohio's last wild cougar was killed long before Miller composed his song. Accounts of that event conflict, one claiming that final extirpation occurred in 1845, while another pegs the date sometime "prior to 1838."[2] Unlike the "yaller" cat of song, however, Buckeye cougars, pumas, mountain lions—call them what you will—simply refuse to disappear.

America's Lion

Cougars (*Puma concolor*) once roamed at large throughout the Western Hemisphere, across the length and breadth of North America, through Mexico and Central America, prowling South America almost to the tip of Tierra del Fuego. Six subspecies are recognized, with the North American cougar (*P. c. couguar*) today including both the eastern cougar (officially deemed extinct by the U.S. Fish and Wildlife Service on March 2, 2011) and the critically endangered Florida panther (sometimes dubbed *P. c. coryi*). West of the Mississippi, cougar sightings are reported regularly, with occasional attacks on humans or their livestock. In Florida, the last verified census of cougars (in 2009) recorded 113 living specimens.[3]

But if eastern cougars are extinct outside of Florida, why do so many people keep seeing them?

Records of the Eastern Puma Research Network list 4,908 cougar sightings east of the Mississippi River from 1950 through 2004. Wildlife authorities dismiss most of those reports, branding cases confirmed from photographs or physical remains as incidents of pets released into the wild, but the EPRN files include 423 sightings of adult cougars with cubs—proof positive, it seems, of breeding populations.[4]

Of those reports collected over 55 years, 135 came from Ohio, including 2 reports of cubs. In fact, Ohio ranked 10th among eastern states reporting cougar sightings, with 118 cases logged between July 1, 1983 and December 31, 2000.[5]

Despite supposed extinction, thousands of cougar sightings are on record from eastern North America.
Credit: U.S. Fish & Wildlife Service

Still, skepticism persists. Official explanations range from exotic pets at large to cases of mistaken identity, even mass hysteria. The media, in general, takes its cue from state authorities, as in a July 2011 article from the *Canton Repository*, reporting a rash of Stark County sightings, maintaining that "there's still no proof."[6]

Or is there?

Multiple Mysteries

It is difficult enough for skeptics to accept the possibility of relict eastern cougar populations in America. What happens, then, when they are asked to swallow tales of mountain lions seen with other cryptids or unidentified flying objects?

One such case was reported from Salem, on the border of Columbiana and Mahoning Counties, in April 1968. Witness Alice Allison allegedly saw an object resembling a black wingless airplane hovering outside her home, above a 30-foot buckeye tree. Inside its lighted dome was "a man [who] wore a khaki-colored shirt. He had olive-colored skin, which was slightly tanned, and his eyes were slanted." After wobbling in place for 20 minutes, the object flew away, but it may have left something behind.[7]

Within a day of the UFO sighting, Mrs. Allison and other members of her family observed an apparent cougar lurking around their property. Sometimes it lounged in their driveway, once leaving 3-inch-wide pawprints after a rainfall. It clawed a nearby tree, leaving scars 6 inches long and half an inch deep, and snarled below their daughter's bedroom window after dark.[8]

Stranger still, the Allisons reported that a hulking manlike figure also occupied the woods around their home. "I don't know what it was," Alice said, "but it was big enough to be a man, a big man. It would stand out in the woods and watch the house. All you could see was a black outline, but it definitely wasn't a bear." Son Bruce saw the biped running through the forest, found depressions in the ground where he suspected it had slept, and blamed it for the disappearance of his tomcat.[9]

Ten years later, on August 21, 1978, Scott Patterson was driving near Minerva, at the juncture of Carroll, Columbiana, and Stark Counties, when he saw two "cougar-type felines" with luminous yellow eyes on the highway ahead. Approaching them, he was astounded when "a large bipedal hairy creature stepped in front of the two cats as if to protect them." It plodded toward his car, whereupon Patterson turned and fled.[10]

What should we make of such accounts? While they defy all logic, I present them here for what they may be worth. The rest of our Ohio cougar sightings, thankfully, are more mundane.

Tracking Phantoms

Ohio resident William Reichling began researching Buckeye cougars in 1988, after he and his son saw one of the cats near their home in Delhi Township. Over the next two years, he found some "could-be tracks," partially devoured opossums, and a dead dog with characteristic bite wounds on the back of its neck. Observing the latter kill over a period of days, he saw a cougar approach the carcass, then flee when it caught his scent. Over the next 16 years, Reichling and his group of R&R Trackers — named for himself and cofounder Dave Reynolds — recorded 86 local eyewitness sightings.[11]

While Reichling's evidence convinced him that the "escaped pet" theory failed to explain cougar sightings, author Bob Butz complained of Reichling's "logical leaps" and "wild theories," deriding photos of claw marks on trees as mere "scratches" and snidely dismissing Ohio's "sketchy history of anecdotal puma sighting(s)." Even so, he grudgingly admitted that Reichling had "clearly found puma scat" and possessed "one unique set of puma tracks in a freshly asphalted parking lot."[12]

At what point does denial shift from honest skepticism to become a hidebound article of faith?

Witness "Paul S." had no doubts concerning the cat he saw, along with his fiancée, pacing along the Ohio River near Cincinnati in October or

November 1997. Tan-gray in color, it stood about 30 inches tall and was at least 5 feet long. Upon spotting them, the cat "slipped back unhurried" into the forest shadows and vanished. The witnesses reported their sighting to Reichling and, they say, "we were asked not to talk about it." Nonetheless, they went public in July 1999.[13]

A final case from the late 1990s did not emerge until March 2004, as an addendum to a Sasquatch report filed with the Bigfoot Field Researchers Organization (BFRO). The unnamed witness was discussing strange encounters with his grandmother, near Minerva in Stark County, when the woman recounted an incident occurring "one summer night [when] she had to close her windows to go to sleep because there was a cougar roaring in the woods. She said she was sure it was some kind of cat."[14]

Strictly speaking, cougars are incapable of "roaring," since they lack the specially adapted larynx and hyoid apparatus found in true "big cats" — members of the genus *Panthera*, including lions, tigers, leopards, and jaguars — but the shrieking cry of a cougar, once heard, is not soon forgotten.[15]

Confrontation and Confusion

The presence of one Buckeye cougar was confirmed on September 21, 2003, when Brian Conway of St. Clairsville shot the cat in self-defense. Police logged several sightings from the neighborhood before the fatal incident, when the cougar attacked farmer Conway's dog, then lunged at him and died from point-blank gunfire. A necropsy revealed that it was surgically declawed, suggesting that it had escaped — or worse yet, been released into the wild, defenseless — by some still-unidentified owner.[16]

There was nothing tame about the cougar residents of Zanesville met ten months later, in July 2004. The predator mauled a pony on July 29, leaving numerous wounds "consistent with that of an attack by another large animal," in the words of attending veterinarian Dr. Mark Atkinson. On the same day, a retired police officer reported his sighting of "a very large cat" to Deputy Chief Wes Elson, saying that it "looked like a mountain lion."[17]

Reports of Muskingum County's cat had begun on July 21, evoking official warnings after the pony attack. Six days later, a cougar left 4-inch-long paw prints near Don Filkill's home, at Hopewell. Eleven sightings were on file by August 10, when Fultonham resident Betty Clayton saw a "humongous" cat cross her front lawn. "It was real reddish looking," she said, "almost like a sorrel horse." By then, the cougar—or some other prowler—had killed a farmer's pygmy goat (on August 6) and a fawn found in a rural driveway (August 11). The *Newark Advocate*, still unimpressed, compared the incidents to "something out of the *Weekly World News*."[18]

That smirking skepticism took a hit on August 31, 2004, when the cougar logged its 21st appearance in Sheriff Bob Stephenson's backyard, on Zanesville's Wesley Chapel Road. Deputies set traps nearby, but the cat had made its point and thus moved on, taunting witness Jeff Flinn the same afternoon. Three more sightings were recorded by September 14, when the cat allegedly killed a dog on Roseville Road. While admitting from descriptions that the beast must be a cougar, authorities still had no luck in trapping it.[19]

Confusion set in two weeks later, with a report from Florida resident Bob Riggle. While visiting in-laws in Zanesville, on September 28, Riggle saw a cat "the size of a large German shepherd, orange in color, with a little white." Unlike a cougar, though, the beast had "hardly any tail." He took it for a bobcat, which may reach 4 feet in length and stand 2 feet tall, but his description fails to match a bobcat's distinctive spotted coat. Riggle's mother-in-law, Louella Smith, also saw the cat and described it as "a lion."[20]

Neighbor Richard Adams disagreed, saying, "There's a real funny-looking dog up on the road there with a real long nose and a real short tail." Sheriff Stephenson encouraged hunters to take their best shot at the cat—or whatever it was—and one hopeful nimrod placed a special mail-order for "wild cat urine," but all in vain. The creature eluded all stalkers and vanished back into limbo.[21]

Here, There, Everywhere
2005-2009

More sightings followed the Muskingum County flap. Motorist Carol Thrasher saw a cougar outside Pemberville, in Wood County, on February 14, 2005. "It came out and stopped right on the road and looked at me and that's when I realized it was a lion." Three-inch paw prints in a nearby muddy field seemed to confirm her opinion.[22]

Rufus Hurst of Granville saw a cougar in his backyard at high noon on December 10, 2005, snapping several photos of the beast as it left paw prints at the scene. His encounter prompted other locals to recall their cougar sightings, dating back to May 2004.[23]

Another motorist, Peggy Hall, was driving near Pataskala, in Licking County, when she spotted a cat "as big as a small deer" beside the highway, on May 7, 2006. "It was very long, very lean, very thin," she said. "It ran so fast, like a greyhound, smooth and sleek. It just took off running real fast. [It was] 8 feet long with a head like a bobcat."[24]

The same cat, or its twin, surfaced 7 months later, on the west side of Columbus, Ohio. Regina Haft saw it from her kitchen window on November 26, estimating that the cougar weighed 120 pounds. "It was beautiful," she said. "It just looked at me and then strolled off. If I was not confident of what I saw, I would not have bothered police. I was concerned because it's a residential area and there are a lot of children and visitors in for the holidays."[25]

Amy Miller of Wilmington was driving to her parents' home in Timber Glen when she met a cougar at roadside, in early January 2007. She said, "It was bigger than a goat, but it wasn't as big as a St. Bernard." The owner of 4 cats, Miller added, "It was not a house cat. It was 7 house cats in one."[26]

In May 2008, Gary Guagenti reported a cougar crossing a field near his home in Shawnee Township, near Lima. An unnamed local told police that he had seen a big cat chasing a deer on June 6, and DNR trapper Craig Shafer acknowledged finding a large felid's tracks in the area, but the cat eluded searchers once again.[27]

Charles and Helen Robertson, residents of Sharon Township on the Medina-Summit County line, logged their first cougar sighting "just before Memorial Day" (May 26) in 2008. In mid-June they found numerous feline paw prints, "both adult and baby ones," in mud near their home. "It was like a highway with all the tracks," said Charles. He saw the large cat on June 25, and again on July 1, that time walking with a cub. The adult, he estimated, measured 3 feet long "from chest to tail" and weighed about 75 pounds. Sheriff's deputies scouted the woods with infrared thermal-imaging gear on August 4, after a neighbor claimed he was attacked by some large beast, but they found nothing.[28]

Sometime in June 2008, ex-policeman Tom Davis and two of his sons saw a cougar stalking miniature horses in a meadow off Southern Road in Creston, on the Medina-Wayne County line. Davis reported the sighting to federal wildlife authorities and was "miffed" at being treated like a kook. Later in the month, he found 6 deer skeletons on his property.[29]

On September 14, 2008, Tom Davis photographed a 5.5-inch feline paw print on his Creston property.[30]

Sue Morgan of Richfield met a cougar on October 3, 2008, while walking her dog on the Lone Pine Golf Course. "It leaped away like a deer," she said, "but it had a long tail that it flipped behind it."[31]

While hunting off Southern Road in Richfield, Rob Grey and his son saw a cougar on October 4, 2008. They delivered stool samples to the U.S. Fish and Wildlife Service, who have yet to release a report of its analysis.[32]

On May 16, 2009, Winter Dryden saw what she believed to be a pair of deer standing near her home at Aberdeen. A moment later, when the object moved, she realized it was a single creature—and, in fact, a large sandy-brown cat. "I stared at it for a minute and it moved its head around, and it was a cat. I saw the tail go out and it was a long, skinny straight tail," she said. "It was very distinctive."[33]

Modern Ohio cougar sightings include reports of cubs.
Credit: U.S. Fish & Wildlife Service

The Deluge

2010-2012

A flood of cougar sightings swamped Ohio as the new century's second decade began. Cases included the following:

January 17, 2010: Stories circulated that a cougar had been killed near Salem, accompanied by emailed photos of the cat's corpse. Local authorities found nothing to support the story and dismissed it as a hoax.[34]

March 25, 2010: Two Cincinnati nursing home employees saw a large tawny cat leap over a 7-foot fence at the Phoenix Community Learning Center. Police turned out in force but found nothing.[35]

May 3, 2010: A resident of Athens reported a "small" cougar lounging on her porch, where it made "gurgling" sounds, then fled into the nearby woods. DNR spokesmen speculated that it was a bobcat.[36]

May 9, 2010: Members of the Rogers family saw and photographed a cougar crossing their property at Gibsonburg, in Sandusky County, prompting a futile police search.[37]

May 19, 2010: Several residents of the Covenant Harbor Retirement Center in Oak Harbor reported a cougar prowling nearby in broad daylight. Police again found nothing.[38]

May 20, 2010: Another Oak Harbor cougar sighting prompted authorities to cancel recess at a nearby school.[39]

May 26, 2010: Brown County sheriff's deputies answered reports of a cougar seen in a field at Georgetown, but failed to spot the animal. On May 27, reports of "a loud growling noise" at a local landfill launched another futile search. Sheriff Dwayne Wenninger subsequently claimed the cougar was purchased by a Mount Orab resident in April, at a Lucasville flea market, then released when it proved aggressive. The negligent buyer remains unidentified, and the cat was not apprehended.[40]

July 17, 2010: A vague report from Cincinnati says that two firefighters saw "a large tan cat" prowling the city's northern suburbs in two separate incidents, 6 months apart. The most recent sighting dated from May 2010, when the cat was seen dragging a deer from a rural highway.[41]

October 19, 2010: Another report without specific details claims that residents of Vinton County, in south-central Ohio, "are seeing mountain lions on their property on a semi regular basis."[42]

October 30, 2010: Spokesmen for Ohio Mountain Lion Watch reported 7 sightings around Athens and Columbus in one week, with two incidents producing photographs. In a third case, a bow hunter saw a cougar pass beneath his tree stand but missed it with two arrows.[43]

December 17, 2010: A family driving north on Interstate 71 reported a pre-dawn cougar sighting. Sadly, while this highway spans the state, no specific location was cited.[44]

December 26, 2010: Ohio Mountain Lion Watch received a sighting report from an unnamed rural community 45 minutes north of Columbus.[45]

December 28, 2010: A resident of northwestern Hamilton County saw "a large tan cat with a long tail" in her fenced backyard, menacing her dog. When she screamed, it leapt over the fence and escaped.[46]

February 12, 2011: Ohio Mountain Lion Watch recorded 5 cougar sightings over the preceding week. Incidents included two separate sightings at Bowling Green's airport in one day; a sighting west of Dayton, near the Indiana border; another at the Clinton Lake Campgrounds, east of Tiffin; and a hunter's claim that he shot and photographed a cougar that rushed his deer stand somewhere "in [the] Adams/Brown County area."[47]

March 8, 2011: The *Daily Jeffersonian of Cambridge* reported "a rash of mountain lion sightings...in recent weeks." Locations included Pleasant City, Seneca Lake, East Cambridge, north of Cambridge, Salt Fork State Park and Larrick Ridge Road, "where multiple sightings have been reported."[48]

April 13, 2011: Muskingum County neighbors Sally Metzger and Sherry Pickens reported a cougar sighting on a farm at New Concord.[49]

April 21, 2011: Guernsey County witness "David" photographed a possible young cougar with a motion-activated camera set beside a game trail near his home, reporting that he also found large paw prints. DNR spokesmen dismissed the creature as "a large domestic cat."[50]

April 23, 2011: A resident of Preble County alerted authorities to a cougar at large. DNR spokesmen reportedly advised a Boy Scout troop to cancel a scheduled campout in the area.[51]

April 29, 2011: A Fayette County farmer emailed photos of a cougar and its paw prints to Ohio Mountain Lion Watch.[52]

June 13, 2011: Several residents of Galloway reported a cougar sighting near Darby Creek.[53]

June 14-26, 2011: An unseen predator killed 4 calves and injured an adult cow on the New Concord farm of Sherry Pickens, where a cougar was seen on April 13. An unnamed "hunter familiar with mountain lions" viewed the wounds and opined that a cougar was responsible.[54]

June 15, 2011: A science teacher from Shadyside High School saw a cougar cross Cash Ridge Road in front of his car. Several students reported sightings prior to the teacher's encounter.[55]

June 18, 2011: Residents of rural Morrow County reported that a "huge tan cat" had terrorized their dog on property near Interstate 71.[56]

June 20, 2011: A resident of rural Hamilton County told police that she saw two cougars roaming her land.[57]

July 2, 2011: Another Hamilton County resident reported a cougar stalking deer along a railroad track by her home, near Cadiz. On the same day, 139 miles to the west, multiple witnesses saw a cougar prowling through Kenton. Local authorities confirmed repeated sightings spanning "several years."[58]

July 4-5, 2011: Police responded to sightings of a cougar roaming at large in Canton. Searches including Ohio State Highway Patrol aircraft failed to locate the animal. Authorities closed Canton's Fairhope Nature Preserve as a precautionary measure, sighting "dozens and dozens of calls" from local witnesses, but the cat remained elusive. On July 8 newspapers published a photo of the animal, snapped by Jeanne Ecrement of Washington Township on June 30, but officials remained skeptical.[59]

July 7, 2011: A Noble County resident reported striking "a large mountain lion cat" with her car. The animal apparently escaped, and while a game warden insisted it must have been a bobcat, the driver maintained that it was "too large" for a normal *Lynx rufus* specimen.[60]

July 8, 2011: A motorist in Fremont saw two "cougar sub adults" playing in a wooded area outside of town. On July 27, she advised Ohio Mountain Lion Watch that her reports to various officials had been "pushed to other departments that never returned her calls."[61]

July 10, 2011: Sightings shifted to Bolivar, in Tuscarawas County, where two locals saw a large cat near their home on Strasburg-Bolivar Road. DNR spokesperson Jamey Graham told reporters, "I'm a firm believer that there is a mysterious feline that's out and about. It's bigger than a big cat, but I don't think it's a mountain lion." No alternative was offered.[62]

July 14, 2011: Authorities in Tuscarawas County received two more reports of cougar sightings. At Newcomerstown, a witness saw a "skinny and malnourished" cat attack and kill a duck, while a state employee in Bolivar saw a healthier-looking specimen roaming around Lawrence Township. Wendell Davenport, a spokesman for Ohio Mountain Lion Watch, told reporters the group had received 10 sighting reports "in the last week alone," excluding reports from Canton.[63]

July 16, 2011: Ohio Mountain Lion Watch logged a report of two cougars seen roaming together on private property at Delhi Township, in Hamilton County.[64]

July 20, 2011: Residents of Perry County reported a cougar sighting.[65]

July 23, 2011: Ohio Mountain Lion Watch logged a trucker's belated report of sighting a cougar on State Route 546, near the 160-mile marker of Interstate 71 in southern Richland County, "around 3 decades ago."[66]

July 24, 2011: A video clip posted to YouTube related the tale of an unnamed man who claimed a cougar attacked him on Canton's southeast side "about a week or so ago." As evidence he displayed a single long scratch on his right forearm.[67]

July 25, 2011: An unnamed hunter reported a cougar sighting two miles outside Kidron, in Wayne County.[68]

July 28, 2011: A Noble County witness reported seeing a "possible sub adult" cougar on State Route 724, 11 miles outside Caldwell. The witness, an experienced woodsman, stated that the animal was not a bobcat, adding that he had "never seen a cat this large."[69]

August 28, 2011: Two bicyclists passed within 20 feet of a hissing cougar on Allen Road, in Stow. One of the witnesses recalled seeing another cougar drinking from a pond along Route 3 in Richfield, two years earlier.[70]

September 2, 2011: A rancher in Anderson Township told authorities that a "big cat" had mauled one of her prize horses, gashing its shoulder and one leg. Previously, a nocturnal predator had killed a rooster and all the farm's hens.[71]

September 3, 2011: While walking his dog at 4:30 a.m., a Camden resident heard "big cat growling sounds" near his home.[72]

September 10, 2011: A Union County couple saw a cougar near their rural home, off State Route 42 between Dublin and Marysville. Prior to the sighting, one of their laying hens was carried off, leaving only scattered feathers.[73]

September 24, 2011: An Amish resident of Holmes County informed Ohio Mountain Lion Watch of local cougar sightings spanning "many years," reported by "very reliable sources."[74]

September 26, 2011: Witnesses reported cougar sightings from Canton and Alliance. On the same day, Ohio Mountain Lion Watch received a two-year-old sighting report from Middletown, accompanied by a purported photo of the cat.[75]

October 12, 2011: Several residents of Browns Run Road, near Middletown, reported cougar sightings. The cat was also caught on film by a motion-activated trail camera.[76]

October 16, 2011: A midnight hunter in Colerain Township saw a cougar on West Kemper Road, in the beam of his Jeep's spotlight.[77]

October 20, 2011: A Lawrence County resident met a cougar near Proctorville, while riding an all-terrain vehicle on a game trail. Later the same day, a couple driving 10 miles east of Zanesville reported an apparent cougar lying dead beside Interstate 70.[78]

November 3, 2011: A bow hunter sighted a cougar on his Milwood Township property, in Guernsey County.[79]

November 4, 2011: Four witnesses traveling on Interstate 675 reported a cougar sighting near Beaver Creek, outside Dayton.[80]

November 11, 2011: Cougar sightings were logged from Oregonia and Washington Courthouse. In the latter incident, a motorist saw "two huge cougars" walking in a ditch beside Interstate 71.[81]

November 15, 2011: A motorist narrowly missed striking a cougar that ran across State Route 63, near Lebanon's Warren Correctional Facility.[82]

December 2, 2011: Ohio Mountain Lion Watch logged a report of "probable" cougar tracks found "several months ago" at Russia, in Shelby County.[83]

December 7, 2011: Witnesses reported a "huge cat" prowling around Salem.[84]

December 12, 2011: A cougar sighting emerged from Belmont County, lacking any details.[85]

December 22, 2011: A motorist traveling south on Interstate 75 near the Franklin exit saw a cougar chasing a white-tailed deer beside the highway.[86]

December 27, 2011: A father and son on their way to shoot targets in Morrow County watched "a massive mountain lion" from a distance, through binoculars. Ohio Mountail Lion Watch reports similar sightings by other local residents.[87]

February 3, 2011: A tourist driving on U.S. Route 23, near Delaware, saw a "huge" cougar prowling along the northbound side of the highway. The witness, an Arizona native long familiar with cougars, insisted there was no mistake in his identification of the cat.[88]

Buckeye cougar sightings have multiplied dramatically in the 21st century. *Credit: U.S. Fish & Wildlife Service*

February 6, 2012: Multiple witnesses claimed an "excellent view of a definite mountain lion" crossing a 200-acre open field near Johnstown, in Licking County.[89]

February 10, 2012: A resident of Cambridge furnished Ohio Mountain Lion Watch with a clear photo of a prowling cougar, caught on a motion-activated trail camera.[90]

February 18, 2012: A motorist reported seeing a cougar at the intersection of State Routes 657 and 661, near Mount Vernon, at 4:00 a.m.[91]

February 20, 2012: A witness saw a cougar near a school bus stop on Portage Trail Road, near Akron's Cuyahoga National Park.[92]

March 13, 2012: Leetonia Police Chief John Soldano warned residents to be alert after a resident sighted a "possible mountain lion" in the alley behind her home on Columbia Street. "We don't want people to panic, but to be aware," Soldano said. "If you do see something, don't try anything yourself. Call the police department." A search for the creature proved futile. [SOURCE: *Salem News*, March 14, 2013.]

June 22, 2012: Ohio Mountain Lion Watch received a cougar sighting report from Lorain County, south of Elyria. An anonymous witness described the cat as "at least knee high, light brown, and the tail was big around and at least as long as the body." [SOURCE: OMLW.]

July 25, 2012: A resident of North Canton glimpsed a cougar outside his 5th Street home, after motion-detector lights in the yard went on at 2:38 a.m. [SOURCE: Action News 19 (Cleveland), August 1, 2012.]

July 27, 2012: Joyce Wise, a resident of North Canton, reported a cougar sighting in her backyard. She described the cat to the Canton Republic as "a light, orangy, tannish color, and [it had] the really long tail that hung all the way to the ground. It was really big, fat and thick and kind of a smallish head and really muscular. When it walked it had really big arms and legs [sic]." That report prompted next-door neighbor Frances Strouble to report a similar sighting, occurring several days before Wise's encounter. [SOURCE: *Canton Republic*, July 27, 2012.]

July 28, 2012: A couple walking on Stark Parks Nature Trail, in North Canton, met "a large tan cat about the size of a German shepherd dog." [SOURCE: Action News 19 (Cleveland), August 1, 2012.]

July 30, 2012: Residents of a home on North Canton's Wilkshire Circle reported "a mountain lion/cougar like animal" passing through their backyard. [SOURCE: Ibid.]

August 2, 2012: After one of his officers photographed a large "cat-like paw print" in North Canton, Police Chief Stephan Wilder told reporters, "We're dealing with something that could be some kind of a hybrid cat or maybe it's a mountain lion. I don't know." [SOURCE: Fox 8 News (Cleveland), August 2, 2012.]

October 5, 2012: Hancock County wildlife officers sought to dispel "rumors" of a cougar prowling around Mount Blanchard, assuring local residents that "it's a cat, but just a really large house cat." Although they never saw the animal, their pronouncement was good enough for Toledo TV reporter Kevin Kistner, who assured his audience that "mountain lions do not live in Ohio." [SOURCE: WNWO Channel 24 (Toledo), October 5, 2012.]

May 12, 2013: A motion-sensitive game camera captured the image of an apparent cougar sitting beside a game trail in Lucas County. [SOURCE: Kentucky Hunting.net, http://www.kentuckyhunting.net/forums/showthread.php?129287-Lucas-County-Ohio-Mountain-Lion-Pic.]

None So Blind...

While it is possible, at least in theory, to explain all of Ohio's modern cougar sightings as encounters with exotic pets lost or released by careless owners, as the number of reported sightings mounts, that view grows tenuous. How many cougars must have been set free within the past two years alone, to account for all the widely-scattered incidents? Conversely, is it feasible that all those witnesses—including seasoned hunters, hikers, and the like—habitually mistake domestic pets or stub-tailed bobcats for much larger, long-tailed cougars?

Consider the following facts:

In South Dakota, where cougars were officially wiped out in 1905, state legislators repealed a ban on hunting the cats in 1999. Four years later, cougars were listed as "big game animals" in the Mount Rushmore State. Fifteen cats, all females, were killed during South Dakota's first official cougar hunting season in 2005, leaving an estimated 165 alive in the wild.[93]

North Dakota, where the "last" wild cougar was reported slain in 1902, also held its first cat-hunting season in 2005, with 5 kills reported by mid-January 2006.[94]

In 2008, Wisconsin wildlife authorities verified the first sighting of a wild mountain lion since the species was officially extirpated in 1908. During the same year — 2008 — Chicago police killed the first wild cougar acknowledged from Illinois since 1855.[95]

On December 14, 2009, deer hunter Raymond Goebels Jr. of Cedar Rapids shot the first cougar verified in Iowa since 1867. He justified the shooting by claiming "it was going to die anyway," and went unpunished since no state law existed protecting the "extinct" species.[96]

In May 2010, Indiana's Department of Natural Resources photographed the first cougar verified in the Hoosier State since the species was officially extirpated, sometime between 1850 and 1865.[97]

The year 2010 also confirmed cougars living wild in Kansas, where they were officially wiped out in 1904. Republican legislator Mitch Holmes quickly proposed a law permitting anyone to kill Kansas cougars without a hunting license, but the measure failed to pass.[98]

With living cougars verified from half a dozen states where they were formerly "extinct," and frequently reported everywhere throughout the eastern United States, how can we justify a stubborn claim that none live in Ohio's wilds?

Indeed, as we shall see in Chapter 3, cougars seem positively tame beside some of the other cats reported prowling through the Buckeye State.

Chapter 3

Feline

Phantoms

On October 18, 2011, mentally unbalanced ex-convict Terry Thompson released 50 exotic animals from his private menagerie near Zanesville, Ohio, then shot himself to death. Sheriff's deputies arrived in response to emergency calls from Thompson's neighbors and reportedly found themselves battling "almost hand to hand" with the frightened, agitated animals. When the gunsmoke cleared, authorities had slaughtered 49 creatures, including 18 Bengal tigers, 17 lions, 6 black bears, 3 cougars, 2 grizzly bears, 2 wolves, and a baboon. One of the lions killed a roaming monkey before police arrived, and another primate—a macaque believed to be infected with the herpes B virus—remained at large. Five animals left in their cages—3 leopards, 2 monkeys, and another grizzly bear—were transported safely to the Columbus Zoo.[1]

Muskingum County Sheriff Matt Lutz told reporters that his records listed "30 to 35 incidents in which we've sent patrol cars to [Thompson's] property since 2004 or 2005 for animals at large, animal cruelty, [and] inhumane treatment of animals." In April 2005, Thompson was charged with torturing cattle and bison at his "preserve." More recently, he had been convicted on weapons charges and sentenced to house arrest. The gruesome incident highlighted Ohio's lax handling of exotic species and prompted passage of new, more restrictive legislation.[2]

While tragic, the Zanesville incident was not Ohio's first case of "alien" big cats roaming at large, and it would not be the last. In fact, reports of unidentified mystery felids predate Thompson's meltdown by at least 134 years.

Black Panthers

As noted in previous series installments, science does not recognize "black panthers" as a species. That common name is interchangeably applied to melanistic jaguars (*Panthera onca*) and leopards (*P. pardus*). While leopards are Old World cats, jaguars are native to the Western Hemisphere, ranging from border areas of the American Southwest through Mexico, Central America, and South America to parts of Argentina, Paraguay, and Peru. Neither cat should logically be found roaming at large in the Midwest.[3]

And yet ....

Unidentified "black panthers" are reported frequently in Ohio.
Credit: U.S. Fish & Wildlife Service

On January 20, 1877, the *New York Times* published an article headlined "A Panther Killed in Ohio," quoting an article from an undated edition of the *Sandusky Register*. According to that article, a nocturnal predator had raided farms around Plymouth Prairie, in Hancock County's New Haven Township, "frequently" killing 40 to 50 sheep in a single night. After "a number of days," local farmers rallied to track the beast and succeeded in killing it "last Friday" — presumably January 12 or 19 — and identifying it as a panther. Fear lingered, as the *Times* explained, because "[I]t is thought that there is still another panther thereabouts — probably the mate of the one that was killed." No further reports were forthcoming.[4]

Nearly two decades passed before the next Buckeye panther's appearance at Lamartine (now Perrysville), a village on the Black Fork Mohican River in Ashland County. Author Loren Coleman dates the sighting from 1895, but offers no further details.[5]

October 1922 brought reports of a curious two-toned panther shrieking in the night around North Woodbury, in Morrow County. Witnesses described the cat as black and white, "about the size of a collie dog," and surmised that it was living in a shack on Zolman's farm, where "a large nest was found" amidst hay. Despite that lead, hunting parties failed to bag their quarry.[6]

Another quarter-century elapsed before Ohio's next panther flap. State highway patrolmen joined civilian hunters on July 10, 1947, to stalk a black cat seen in Bloomfield Township. That hunt was still ongoing in September, when the panther killed a calf at Parkman, in neighboring Geauga County, on September 10. As usual, the beast eluded its pursuers.[7]

On August 22, 1948, Darke County game warden Robert Wiegand announced that a black panther was "probably loose" around Greenville, perhaps a fugitive from some unspecified circus or carnival. Witness Daisy Mills had seen the animal outside New Madison, insisting that it "definitely was not a dog." In early September, "unusual tracks" were found at Morning Sun, in nearby Preble County.[8]

A partial solution for recent panther sightings emerged from Butler County's Fairfield Township on July 18, 1949. Local farmers had scoured the district for a nocturnal predator, firing close-range shots before the beast escaped on July 14. They found it dead near Tylersville 4 days later, describing their kill as "a large, nearly-black bobcat" that measured 4 feet long, weighed about 150 pounds, "and had fangs and claws as long as a man's fingers." The latter bit was clearly wild exaggeration, and the cat's supposed weight nearly quadruples the record for a male of the species. As for more traditional long-tailed panthers reported from Ohio's wilds, newspapers of the era speculated that "black leopards" may have been imported by Mexican migrant workers and raised as pets, then released to breed in the wild.[9]

Whether or not Butler County's bobcat qualified as a "panther," its death did not end reports of still larger black cats on the prowl. The Byrd brothers of Mansfield were hunting rabbits on November 23, 1950, when they saw a 4-foot-long creature they labeled "a giant black tomcat."[10]

That sighting may be the first of 31 Ohio panther reports logged by the Eastern Puma Research Network between 1950 and 2005, though details from those files are not readily available.[11] Other known encounters from that era include:

July 1953: Witness Bert Giaque reported the first of several Holmes County panther sightings 3 weeks before the creature's existence rated mention in the *Van Wert Times-Bulletin* of July 31. Hunters failed to bag the cat.[12]

August 6, 1956: Multiple witnesses saw a black, long-tailed "catlike" creature prowling along State Route 13 between Florence and Birmingham. Paw prints were found, but the creature escaped.[13]

December 21, 1958: Elmer Griffith saw a black panther 3 miles north of a Northern Ohio Power and Light substation on State Route 25, at Lima. Two witnesses, Katherine Early and an unidentified motorist, claimed separate panther sightings near the power station on December 23.[14]

January 9, 1959: The *Van Wert Times-Bulletin* claimed that a farmer in Convoy had killed and skinned a large black cat that mauled his dog. Local fur dealer

Albert Pancake bought the pelt for $75 and pronounced it a black cougar's. Ten days later, the *Lima News* reported multiple sightings of another panther prowling around Van Wert.[15]

1959: In March 2005, the *Cleveland Plain Dealer* asserted that a panther "stalked Lorain County in 1959." The article supplied no further details.[16]

May 19, 1961: Three Elyria residents reported a black panther traipsing along State Routes 10 and 20. Kathryn Roll saw the cat near State Route 82, on May 24, and members of the Charles Zalenka family blamed it for mauling their dog on May 25.[17]

May through July 1962: Author Loren Coleman reports "a major 'black panther' flap" around Urbana, in Champaign County. More than a dozen witnesses claimed sightings of the cat, and one emerged to say that he had seen it west of town in 1955, as well.[18]

January 1, 1963: Max Allen of South Salon chased a panther in his pickup truck and fired 9 shots at it before the cat escaped. Over the next week, several other witnesses claimed sightings near the county seat at London, including discovery of 5-inch-wide paw prints.[19]

August 8, 1964: The *Mansfield News Journal* reported that a panther "sporadically seen over the past 5 years" had returned to maul two horses at Minerva, leaving claw marks on their flanks.[20]

March 22, 1977: A black cat described as "about 3 feet long and 24 to 30 inches in height, weighing 100 to 125 pounds" killed several sheep and left others wounded on Elmer Nesbaum's farm, in Allen County's Richland Township. It returned on March 26, springing 6 traps, scarring a wooden fence, and leaving more sheep injured with "8 perfect claw marks" on their flanks. Sherman Burkholder lost 57 sheep in two successive raids, on the nights of April 25 and 26. Maria Henderson was first to see the cat, on April 28, and more sightings followed. By May 21 the death toll stood at 140 sheep and 1 German Shepherd. Despite eyewitness descriptions of the panther, Sheriff Charles Harrod blamed the killings on feral dogs. When witness William Reeder, executive director of the Allen County Humane Society, publicly disagreed, Sheriff Harrod forbade him from speaking to the press.[21]

May 1979: Panther sightings began around Westerville, on the Delaware-Franklin County line. On June 10, Charles and Helen Marks found more than 200 large feline paw prints around their home.[22]

November 30, 1984: Lillian Smith reported her first meeting with a black panther in Cincinnati's North Avondale neighborhood, followed by another sighting on December 2. Police sergeant Alan Jones told reporters, "I have some doubts, but we have had a lot of reports from people and we are not discounting the stories." Three-inch-wide paw prints were found at a local high school, and researcher Ron Schaffner writes that "reports of the animal persisted for a couple of years."[23]

1984: Cleveland's *Plain Dealer* says that a panther visited North Olmsted during this year, but provides no details.[24]

October 1989: Howard Appling and another witness logged separate sightings of a large black cat in Ottawa County's Carroll Township. Unnamed spokesmen for unidentified "local zoos" examined casts of the creature's paw prints and "speculated it might be a large dog."[25]

2001: Four years after the fact, the *Plain Dealer* reported that a "big panther-like animal put a scare into southern Medina County." No further details were forthcoming.[26]

May 2, 2004: Responding to the panicked barking of his dog, Donald Nason saw a black panther near his home on East Harbor Road, in Ottawa County's Portage Township. Within a single article, the *Port Clinton News Herald* called the cat a black panther, a "puma-like creature," and an "alleged lion," finally settling on "a dark unidentified beast."[27]

June 15, 2004: A resident of Danbury Township found large feline paw prints along Bayshore Road. Motorist Joleen Gracemyer nearly struck a large black cat with her car at 12:30 a.m. the next day, and her fiancé saw the animal less than two hours later. Neighbor Derek Chambers logged a sighting from his Bayshore Road home the same day. Again, the *Port Clinton News Herald* termed the cat both a "black panther" and a "puma."[28]

December 10, 2005: Rufus Hurst, his wife and sister saw and videotaped a large black cat on their wooded property in Granville. Measurement between paw prints revealed a 3-foot stride. Two police officers glimpsed the panther on December 12, seeming unimpressed when DNR spokesman Dan Huss dismissed it as "a very large house cat." On December 13, police delivered printed warnings of "a small danger" to local residents from "a large wild cat" at large.[29]

January or February 2007: DNR officers received multiple reports of a panther roaming near Wapakoneta and Breese Roads, in Lima.[30]

November 2007: A deer hunter spotted a panther on State Route 309, between Delphos and Elida.[31]

June 4, 2008: A Lima resident reported a panther at large downtown, at the corner of Woodlawn and Market Streets. Police found nothing.[32]

April 2011: Tim Harrison, director of the Dayton-based group Outreach for Animals, reported the latest of 3 recent panther sightings from the local area, identifying the still-at-large creature as a "black leopard."[33]

June 5, 2011: Ohio Mountain Lion Watch logged a report of a panther sighted on Dayton property owned by the Boy Scouts of America.[34]

July 16, 2011: Residents of Harrison reported two separate "close encounters" with a black panther.[35]

August 29, 2011: Chris Walton saw a panther weighing 160 to 200 pounds outside his home on Lofty Oaks Lane, in Dayton. The *Daily News* reported a second sighting by an unnamed witness on September 1.[36]

September 26, 2011: A couple in Nelsonville watched a panther leap over a fence near their home.[37]

October 13, 2011: Police investigated a woman's report of a panther sitting outside her apartment in Strongsville. The cat was gone when they arrived.[38]

October 22, 2011: A resident of New Carlisle reported a panther sunning itself in a hayfield. James Mitchell of Pike Township logged another encounter on October 25. Tim Harrison viewed the second animal's tracks and pronounced himself "98-percent sure" a big cat was at large.[39]

December 10, 2011: Tim Harrison viewed photos of a black felid seen in German Township, declaring it "more likely a housecat than a panther."[40]

February 9, 2012: Ohio Mountain Lion Watch received a Dayton resident's report of a "huge black cat" making repeated kills on his property since June 2011, with blood and paw prints found.[41]

February 20, 2012: A resident of Delhi Township saw a "large black cat" walking along U.S. Route 50. Ohio Mountain Lion Watch says similar sightings "have been recorded for many years from many reputable sources."[42]

Leopards at Large

Eleven months after the *New York Times* reported a black panther's demise in Hancock County, in November 1877, a leopard panicked residents of Marion County, 40 miles to the southeast. Shot by hunters near New Bloomington on December 1, the cat reportedly had escaped from a railroad car near Mansfield, in June, while en route "to some Geological Garden."[43]

LaRue, also in Marion County, witnessed another leopard hunt in November 1895, with the first sighting logged by two hunters on November 23. A local farmer claimed two sightings in Marseilles Township, on November 25, and while a posse beat the bushes, finding 3 hogs slain, the cat escaped. Marion's Star ran the story with a headline reading "This May Be A Lie."[44]

Yet another spotted cat appeared near Portsmouth, in Scioto County, attacking farmer Fred Klefford and one of his hired hands in December 1906. The *Portsmouth Times* compared it to "Pasha," a leopard on tour with Frank Bostock's traveling menagerie, but suggestions of Pasha's escape proved groundless and the predator eluded hunting parties.[45]

Ohio leopard sightings date from the 19th century.
Credit: U.S. Fish & Wildlife Service

King of Beasts

Old World lions have been frightening Ohio residents for over half a century. The first appeared outside Cincinnati on New Year's Day 1936. A witness identified only as "Miller" fired at the cat from his window, but missed. Police confirmed his sighting from paw prints in snow "and soggy ground," but never saw the lion.[46]

Summer 1959 witnessed the slaughter of domestic pets and livestock by a "huge cat" in Lorain County. According to Loren Coleman, witnesses described the predator as looking "somewhat like a miniature 'African' lion," complete with bushy mane.[47]

Another lion surfaced in Groesbeck, in 1971. Loren Coleman reported that the cat "disappeared as quickly as it came," but offers no further details. (He also spelled the town's name as "Croesbeck.")[48]

On September 4, 1975, a Coshocton mechanic met a "lion" outside his garage. The cat stood 3 feet tall, weighed about 250 pounds, and fled before police arrived. Loren Coleman cites a *Cleveland Plain Dealer* article suggesting the cat had a mane, but the *Coshocton Tribune* specifically denied this, suggesting that the beast may have been a cougar.[49]

Reports of lions at large in Ohio continue to the present day.
Credit: U.S. Fish & Wildlife Service

Irish author Ronan Coghlan mentions an Ohio lion seen in 1977, citing Loren Coleman's *Mysterious America* as his source, but that volume's only reference to a Buckeye mystery cat from that year involves the black panther seen between March and May (see above).[50]

In August 1979, a resident of Butler County's West Chester Township found a lion cub outside his back door. Authorities traced the young cat to an "amusement company," from where it had escaped.[51]

North Olmsted, described by Loren Coleman as "apparently a very wild Cleveland suburb," produced a lion sighting in July 1984. Details are lacking, but the town — with a population density of 2,933 residents per square mile in 2000 — hardly qualifies as wilderness.[52]

Four months later, lion sightings emerged from North Avondale, a neighborhood near downtown Cincinnati. Reports continued through December, but police could not locate the cat.[53]

Police in Mentor logged multiple sightings of a male lion during June 1992. Witnesses were adamant in their descriptions of the maned cat, 7 feet long, with "big shoulders," but authorities decreed that they had seen a "large golden retriever."[54]

Confusing reports of one or more mystery cats emerged from Highland and Clinton Counties in November 1994. A Salem Township resident was first to call police, on November 10, reporting a "tan-and-white" striped cat she described as a "tiger." Moments later, Chris Hawk reported a "big and brown" felid racing across her nearby property. Later that night, Clara Stroop heard and saw a cat resembling "a cougar or a female lion" roaring outside her mobile home. Paw prints from two sighting locations proved to be identical. On November 19, Lynchburg motorist Lance Lukas nearly struck a large cat on Anderson Road, in Dodson Township, describing its coat as "tannish-yellow... like a leopard without spots." The flap ended there, with the beast still unidentified.[55]

On June 29, 2003, Casper Lawson saw a lion on his farm, in Warren County's Deerfield Township. The cat appeared twice more before he phoned police, on July 3, including an encounter wherein nephew Charlie Lawson saw the beast "real plain" at close range. Officers turned out in force, with helicopters and tracking dogs, but found only "rather indiscernible tracks of something," as described by an expert from the Cincinnati Zoo. Deputies accused Casper Lawson of lying, subjecting him to a "voice stress test" at headquarters, but he stuck with his story. "We'll catch it," he promised reporters. "I'm going to see to it one way or another."[56]

On May 3, 2004, police in the Columbus suburb of Gahanna warned residents to stay indoors to avoid meeting a 400-pound "exotic cat" on the prowl. Deputy Chief Larry Rinehart named one of his officers as the first witness, with a second sighting logged by courier service employee Jack Dingess. By May 4, authorities had logged 11 sightings of an "African lion" in the neighborhood, rating 3 reports as "credible." Hunters saw a coyote that day, but missed the cat. Authorities speculated on May 5 that the beast might be a deer, but fresh lion sightings emerged on May 6. "Giant paw prints" appeared at the Jefferson Country Club's golf course on May 9, but a Columbus Zoo spokesman declared that "a lion did not likely make the prints." Officials at Kirkersville Elementary School canceled recess on May 12, after sightings of a beast "larger than a dog" and "too big for a kitty."[57]

Gahanna's lion soon expanded its range. A resident of Hebron saw it near her home on May 12, but it evaded sheriff's deputies. On June 25, Gahanna police lieutenant Jeff Spence told reporters, "We're putting the lion in the cold case squad," but the story still had legs. Firefighter Ed Dildin saw the cat in Franklin County's Madison Township on July 8, describing it as "about 200 pounds and blond, with a sleek body and long tail." He added, "I promise you it was a lion." Dildin's sighting was the second in as many days, with a third logged from the same vicinity on July 10. Don and Sherry Filkill found a large paw print on the same day at their property in Hopewell. Sheriff's Lieutenant Jeff LeCocq confirmed the find, but could not decide if the track belonged to lion or cougar.[58]

Thirteen months before Granville's first black panther sighting, on November 3, 2004, resident Anne Russell saw a lion in a field near the intersection of Cherry Valley and Newark-Granville Roads. Responding officers briefly glimpsed a "large cat-like animal with a large, round, beige-colored head," seemingly unfazed by their flashlights and radio chatter. On November 15, Dan Gartner and Holly Hanbaum reported the cat lounging in a tree, in their backyard, but it was gone when police reached the home near Ohio State University's Newark campus.[59]

On January 1, 2005, Marc Trombino and his mother glimpsed what they thought was a deer, while driving on U.S. Route 40 near Mill Dam Road. A closer look through fog revealed a "very muscular" cat, about 6½ feet long, "black and gray, perhaps covered with mud, with a ridge of hair from its head down to its shoulders."[60]

Ohio's last reported lion sighting — so far — occurred northwest of Sunbury in late December 2006. Motorist Don Anderson saw the cat running across a golf course under construction beside Wilson Road. The tan cat was "really booking," he said, and cleared the two-lane road in a single bound, without touching asphalt. Size and color aside, its gait reminded Anderson of a cheetah chasing prey at top speed.[61]

Tigers by the Tail

On June 1, 1994, Debbie Couch saw "a large orange animal" run across State Route 471 near Springboro, disappearing into woods beside the runways of Dayton General Airport South (now Dayton International). Authorities responded and found nothing, but recorded Couch's description of an apparent Bengal tiger.[62]

Five months later, as described above, a resident of nearby Salem Township reported another "tiger" sighting, muddled by subsequent reports of a big cat resembling a lion. Again, the beast escaped.[63]

Ohio's last tiger report before the Zanesville massacre may represent a case of mistaken identity. Clair Dunbar of Medina logged the sighting on April 4, 2001, after a large striped cat appeared in his backyard. Neighbor Meghan Williamson quickly advised police that a savannah cat—the hybrid offspring of a domestic cat and an African serval (*Leptailurus serval*)—had escaped from her care while she was house-sitting for friends. She asked nervous locals to spare the cat's life, while Dunbar admitted that he may have "overshot the weight a bit" in his description to police.[64]

Modern Ohio legislation restricts—but does not ban—private ownership of tigers.
Credit: U.S. Fish & Wildlife Service

Something Else

Aside from recognizable exotics, Ohio has produced many reports of "wildcats" bearing sparse resemblance to any known species. The first frightened berry-pickers Artie Selmon, John Selmon, and Milton Woods at a site 3 miles east of Washington Court House in early August 1921. Police searched in vain, but found large tracks that "showed plainly that the animal was some species of the cat family." Richmond's *Gazette* declared that the region's last "wildcat" was killed nearby, "several years ago."[65]

R. E. Holskey of Coshocton was walking his dog along State Route 76 on May 30, 1944, when he found a strange cat apparently killed by passing traffic. It was brownish-gray, measured 40 inches long and 20 inches high at the shoulder, with fangs three-quarters of an inch long and a tail "too long to be the tail of a bobcat." Local clergyman M. S. Kanaga thought the creature was "a young lynx," though it nearly rivaled record measurements for an adult of that species (also known for its stubby tail).[66]

On December 8, 1946, Fred Laman shot a long-tailed cat on his farm near Allentown. It was gray, measured 31.5 inches, and weighed 11 pounds. Its coat was dark gray, with darker stripes on the legs. Lima's *News* considered it "a sister to one which was shot a month ago in the same neighborhood," also unidentified.[67]

Lorain and Preble Counties suffered a mystery cat flap in May 1959, with various sightings reported from Avon, Columbia, Eaton, North Ridgeville, and Wellington. Descriptions varied widely: Anne Kozel saw a bushy-tailed creature "a little larger than a tomcat," while possessing "the biggest cat head I ever saw." George Hricovec noted a smooth tail "with a tuft on the end," and a third witness said the beast was "larger than his large dog." Game wardens examined a slaughtered dog and pronounced the paw prints near its body to be canine. By the time Fortean author Brad Steiger described the case in *Beyond Reality*, 16 years later, the creature had become "[a] giant cat with a large head...reported to be consuming dogs, cats, and sheep. One woman found 6 of her sheep literally ripped apart. One was completely skinned and another was missing."[68]

On January 14, 1966, Don Miller's column in the *Elyria Chronicle Telegram* reported that local hunters had killed a "long-tailed wild cat," described as young and furry, with an 8-inch tail resembling a raccoon's, a striped gray pelt, and "big heavy feet" with sharp claws. While personally mystified, Miller accepted a wildlife officer's suggestion to "mark it down as a feral domesticated cat."[69]

Ronan Coghlan reports that a gray-and-black cat of unknown species visited Millersport sometime in 2001, adding: "It has been suggested that the animal was not a cat, but a coyote."[70] My search of his online source (Cryptozoology.com) revealed no corresponding article.

On March 25, 2010, Cincinnati police, firefighters, and animal rescue workers turned out in force to stalk a "large white cat" seen prowling through suburban Avondale. Described without explanation as "a tiger" in the *Cincinnati Enquirer*, the animal eluded pursuit.[71]

Four months later, on July 13, Rose Wingert saw "a rare type of cat" outside her home in Granville. It was not a cougar, she insisted, but "a lean and long animal" with a long tail and a mottled coat in shades of brown and gray covering its 3-foot-long body. Andrew Montoney, speaking for the U.S. Department of Agriculture's Wildlife Services in Reynoldsburg, ruled out any feline species native to Ohio, suggesting that Wingert may have seen a coyote, fox, or some exotic cat.[72]

A motorist in Hamilton County's Colerain Township sighted a cat of unknown species on the morning of August 5, 2011. Based on his description, spokesmen for Ohio Mountain Lion Watch speculated that it may have been a jaguarundi (*Puma yagouaroundi*), a wild cat native to Central and South America.[73]

Eight weeks later, on September 30, a retired teacher sighted a cat "bigger than [her] St. Bernard dog" near her home in Clarksville. Its gray pelt featured "possible stripes," while its size convinced the witness not to leave her home alone at night.[74]

Questions of Identity

How do we explain Ohio's mystery cats? Exotic escapes and releases undoubtedly account for some modern cases, but the farther back we go in time, the less likely we are to find a thriving big-cat trade. In certain cases, feline refugees from carnivals or circuses have been suggested as the culprits, but despite vague allusions to some unidentified traveling show — and a single, seemingly erroneous reference to Frank Bostock's itinerant menagerie in 1906 — that solution remains hypothetical. Likewise, suggestions that slave-traders brought African cats to America before the Civil War are purely speculative.

Reviewing cases of American "black panthers," author Chad Arment suggests some other possibilities that may, in fact, apply to other mystery felids as well. They include:

Misidentification. Black dogs and atypically large domestic cats might be mistaken for panthers at a distance or in woodlands, by a startled witness. In the same way, a cougar and "African" lioness might be confused.

Hoaxes. Deliberate fraud may explain some reports in this age where, it seems, some damaged souls will do anything to get attention.

Melanistic cougars. Reports of black or nearly-black cougars throughout the Americas have been recorded since the 18th century, with several accounts of specimens killed in Latin America—and one allegedly shot in Colorado, in December 1912. Despite those claims, and the assumption of some researchers that North American "panthers" must be melanistic cougars, no confirmed black specimens are presently recognized by science.[75]

Relict species. Authors Loren Coleman and Mark Hall raise yet another possibility: survival of the prehistoric North American lion (*Panthera leo atrox*), identified in 1853 from fossil remains and presumed extinct for some 11,000 years. The largest known specimen *Panthera leo atrox* weighed about 774 pounds, with the average male's weight pegged around 563 pounds. Reconstructions of the cat reveal no mane on either males or females, but Coleman and Hall posit that males were maned, further suggesting that sexual dimorphism might produce black females, thus explaining occasional sightings of "African" lions prowling in company with "black panthers."[76]

It goes without saying that mainstream science rejects any suggestion of *Panthera leo atrox's* survival into modern times, just as many wildlife "experts" east of the Mississippi refuse to consider the prospect of cougars living and breeding in the wild. The mystery remains unsolved.

Chapter 4

In Cold Blood

Reptiles — with their close relatives, amphibians — repel and fascinate mankind in roughly equal measure. Some possess deadly venom, while others grow to awesome size and count humans among their dietary staples. Ohio is home to 45 native reptile species and 39 amphibians, yet reports logged across 4 centuries suggest that other species, some of truly remarkable size, may also trace their roots to Buckeye soil.

In the Pink

Our one and only tale of an apparent cryptic amphibian comes from Scippo Creek, in Pickaway County. The report is vague on dates, referring merely to the "early 1800s," clarified by author Mark Hall as referring to some time before 1820. Although initially described as pink lizards ranging from 3 to 7 feet in length, the creatures were invariably seen in or near water, suggesting an amphibian identity. That theory is supported by eyewitness descriptions of the "lizards" sporting antlers "like a moose," surmised by Hall to be external gills displayed by certain salamander species. Around 1820, successive droughts and wildfires destroyed most of the creatures' wetland habitat and apparently caused their extinction.[1]

Nearly two-thirds of Ohio's amphibian species are salamanders, the largest on record being the hellbender (*Cryptobranchus alleganiensis*), with a record length of 29 inches. A close competitor, the totally aquatic mudpuppy (*Necturus maculosus*), may exceed 19 inches. While hellbenders rank as North America's largest known salamander (and third-largest in the world), mudpuppies have bright-red, branching external gills that might be mistaken for horns by a witness unfamiliar with the species. Mudpuppy gills aside, neither species is known for pink or red coloration.[2]

Science recognizes two much larger salamander species: the Chinese giant salamander (*Andrias davidianus*), with a record 6-foot length, and the Japanese giant salamander (*A. japonicus*), known to approach 5 feet. Neither displays the "antler" gills described from Scippo Creek, and none should normally be found in North America.[3]

A Buckeye Dinosaur?

The late 19th century produced another big lizard report, this one apparently describing a reptilian specimen. No date is provided beyond "the late 1800s" for this encounter near Crosswick, in Warren County. Two boys were fishing at a creek when a huge "snake" approached, then sprouted legs and grabbed one of the youths, dragging him toward a large hollow tree downstream. Workmen at a nearby quarry heard the boys screaming and ran to their rescue, whereupon the creature dropped its prey and ducked inside the tree, described as 26 feet in diameter. Reports differ as to whether the injured boy survived or died.[4]

Naturally alarmed, the rescuers organized a party of 60 men, equipped with hunting dogs and axes, and returned to kill the beast. As they hacked at the tree, it emerged, rising on its hind legs to a height of 12 feet or more, and fled in that manner for a mile, until it vanished down a burrow in a rocky hillside. Witnesses described the animal as being "from 30 to 40 feet long, and 16 inches in diameter, and the legs 4 feet long and covered with scales, as was the body. The feet, about 12 inches long and shaped like a lizard's, were of black and white color with large yellow spots. The head was about 16 inches wide with a long, forked tongue, and the mouth was deep red inside. The hind legs appeared to be used to give an erect position, and its propelling power is in its tail." Researcher Nick Sucik writes that 3 witnesses saw a similar creature "some years later," crossing a road near a swamp east of Lebanon, but admits that "details are lacking."[5]

The Crosswick beast sounds like a monitor lizard in all respects except its size, which is triple to quadruple that of the largest known living species. Some smaller monitors do run on their hind legs when frightened, although larger specimens apparently do not. A prehistoric ancestor, *Megalania*, exceeded 20 feet in length, but its fossil remains have only been found in Australia, where it presumably died out some 40,000 years ago.[6]

While smaller monitor lizards may be found in Ohio as exotic pets, the state boasts only 5 native species of lizards. The largest is the broad-headed skink (*Eumeces laticeps*), with a record length of 17 inches.[7]

The Crosswick beast surpassed Earth's largest known lizard in size.
Credit: U.S. Fish & Wildlife Service

Snakes Alive!

Ohio claims 28 native snake species, all but 3 of them harmless. Largest among them is the black rat snake (*Pantherophis obsoletus*), known by many alternative names, with a record length of 8 feet, 5 inches. The timber rattlesnake (*Crotalus horridus*) boasts a record length of 6 feet, 2 inches, while 2 species of racer — black (*Coluber constrictor priapus*) and blue (*C. c. foxii*) — tie for third place at a maximum 6 feet. The rare eastern fox snake (*Elaphe gloydi*) comes in fourth, at 4 feet, 5 inches.[8]

The exotic pet trade explains most modern reports of pythons found at large in urban areas, although, as we shall see, Ohio has produced many reports of much larger serpents, spanning three centuries. Before examining the giants, though, we should investigate the strange case of venomous coral snakes found in the state.

Ohio's 3 recognized venomous species are all pit vipers (subfamily *Crotalinae*): the timber rattler, the eastern massassauga (*Sistrurus catenatus catenatus*), and the northern copperhead (*Agkistrodon contortrix mokeson*). Coral snakes (family *Elapidae*) are found worldwide, with more than 80 recognized species. At least 3 species are native to the United States, ranging from the Carolinas westward to Texas and Arizona, but none are recognized as living wild in Ohio.[9]

Nonetheless, in 1892, the Cincinnati Society of Natural History reported that Dr. John Warder of North Bend had given the society's museum a coral snake caught somewhere in Ohio, sometime earlier. A second specimen was captured in 1944, in Cincinnati's Price Hill neighborhood, where efforts to identify it as an escaped pet proved fruitless. Author Chad Arment notes that several harmless species mimic brightly-colored coral snakes in appearance, although none is native to Ohio.[10]

While researching the subject, Arment collected 5 more reports of apparent coral snakes from Buckeye witnesses.

Arment's own cousin saw "a small brightly banded snake" unlike any known Ohio species in Highland County, date unknown.[11]

A former Boy Scout recalled seeing a similar specimen near Delaware "about 17 years ago," but could not recall "if it was red, black, and yellow or red, yellow, and black."[12] Yellow or white bands separate black and red bands on North American coral snakes, while adjacent red and black bands indicate a harmless species.

A surveyor was "pretty sure" that he saw — and stepped on — a coral snake near Mount Gilead in August 1998.[13]

Another witness "got a real good look" at 2 apparent coral snakes, swimming in a creek near Mentor, describing both as 10 inches long.[14]

Clockwise from above:

The black rat snake is Ohio's largest recognized species of snake.
Credit: U.S. Fish & Wildlife Service

Venomous coral snakes normally live far south of Ohio.
Credit: U.S. Fish & Wildlife Service

Scarlet king snakes mimic corals, but their red and yellow bands do not touch.
Credit: U.S. Fish & Wildlife Service

One last witness reported a childhood encounter with a brightly-banded snake at Cincinnati, "27 years ago," but was uncertain whether it had been a coral or a scarlet kingsnake (*Lampropeltis elapsoides*), also officially foreign to Ohio.[15]

During the course of his research, Arment also found two witnesses who claimed sightings or captures of scarlet kingsnakes on 4 separate occasions. One claimed he caught 2 specimens at Camp Lazarus, a Boy Scout facility in Delaware County, between 1983 and 1987. The other witness saw 2 of the snakes, one in Guernsey County, the other at an unnamed youth camp somewhere in southern Ohio. Scarlet kings are found in northern Kentucky, and Arment speculates that some may find their way farther north.[16]

They Might Be Giants

Exotic snakes surface in Ohio's urban jungles with some regularity, the largest on record being a 14-foot reticulated python (*Python reticulatus*) caught in Cincinnati on August 17, 2011.[17] Those cases may be simply explained as exotic pets gone astray, but what do we make of reports dating back to the 18th century, describing giant reptiles unlike any species known to science?

Our first report comes from the June 1795 issue of Rutland, Vermont's *Rural Magazine*, describing an "American anaconda." After first misplacing that New World reptile (genus *Eunectes*) in Ceylon (now Sri Lanka), the article claimed that a specimen was killed by hunters west of Fort Recovery on May 27, 1793. The snake measured 26 feet, 7.5 inches long and was marked with "streaks of bright red, green, white, purple, and pale blue, more beautiful than can be well imagined" — in short, nothing at all like a true anaconda. When cut open, it allegedly contained "a panther, several squirrels of different species, birds, insects, and snakes of an inferior kind, all of which had been swallowed whole, and not a bone broken." Its skin, supposedly, was on display at "the Philadelphia museum."[18]

On January 31, 1846, an Illinois newspaper reported that 6 "respectable citizens" of Clermont County had signed an affidavit confirming their encounter with a snake "full 30 feet" long, seen in a pond near Batavia.[19]

John Wait, also of Batavia, signed his own affidavit before a justice of the peace on August 11, 1849, stating that he saw a snake at least 30 feet long in a local mill-pond, on August 1. Its eye was "about as large as the mouth of a tea-cup." Searches ensued, involving 400 to 500 hunters, but no serpent was found.[20]

South American anacondas are not native to Sri Lanka — or to Ohio. *Credit: U.S. Fish & Wildlife Service*

August 1865 brought reports of an "anaconda" seen crawling beside the Pittsburgh, Cincinnati, Chicago, and St. Louis Railroad tracks between Newcomerstown and Port Washington. Coshocton's *Democrat* initially treated the sightings as a hoax, until New Philadelphia's *Ohio Democrat* declared the beast "as much of a verity as ever the great sea serpent was." A witness who saw the reptile in a tree, on August 22, compared it to a giant copperhead (record length: 4 feet, 5 inches).[21]

On October 6, 1868, the *Ohio Democrat* reported that a "very large" snake had been frequently seen for a year on the Kirk farm, two miles west of Barnesville. Witness James Woodland claimed several encounters with the reptile, most recently on September 15. It was black, he said, at least 30 feet long, and 10 inches thick.[22]

A smaller snake, 16 feet long, was reportedly shot at the Crittenden farm, outside Columbus, on July 8, 1869. Despite a claim that "the skin will be stuffed and brought to this city" (Columbus), no trace of it remains.[23]

Just 3 months later, on October 29, someone killed a black snake of unknown species, 11 feet, 2 inches long, at Sharon. North America's largest native snake species, the bullsnake (*Pituophis catenifer sayi*), claims a record length of 8 feet, 9 inches and is not black.[24]

The *Ohio Democrat's* next item, from July 28, 1871, is an apparent "silly season" hoax. It describes a 15-foot snake prowling Carroll County's Perry Township, claiming the serpent had "already swallowed an old gray horse, a lot of children, and a mowing machine."[25]

A more serious report from Elyria's *Independent Democrat* describes the slaying of large snake near Loudonville on August 12, 1872. The snake measured 23 feet, 3 inches and was "supposed to be one of the number that has infested Jerome[s]ville for years."[26]

Joseph Selby of Barnesville was picking raspberries in early August 1873, when he sat on a log to rest and felt it move beneath him. It proved to be a snake, 50 to 60 feet long and as thick as Selby's torso, presumably the same serpent seen by others "for several years past."[27]

Multiple sightings surfaced in July 1874. George Churchill and a second Dallas Township witness, one "Robert," quarreled over whether they had seen 1 or 2 snakes, 12 to 15 feet long. A third person, "Old Holmes," allegedly shot a blue racer 13 feet, 4 inches long on Independence Day, in neighboring Marion County, but hogs devoured the carcass before he could skin it.[28]

On July 24, 1876, the *New York Times* quoted an article from Ashtabula's *Telegraph*, concerning a 20-foot snake seen by Thomas Manning near the Lake Shore and Michigan Southern Railway line. Armed hunters returned to the site but found nothing.[29]

The *Times* carried another report on August 8, 1878, from the *Sandusky Register*. A snakeskin 9 feet long and 19 inches wide, recently shed, had been found on a farm in Perkins Township. Its markings prompted speculation that it came from a Latin American boa (*Boa constrictor*), one of a pair that had escaped two years earlier from a traveling menagerie at Milan, on the Erie-Huron County line.[30]

On August 14, 1879, the *Athens Messenger* cited a "well authenticated story" from Cleveland's *Leader*, regarding a snake killed at Nevada, Ohio. It was 21 feet, 2.5 inches long and measured 19.5 inches in circumference.[31]

Two years later, on June 22, 1881, a Maryland newspaper announced that settlers living along Williams Creek, near Rockville, had been terrorized by a dark-brown snake at least 20 feet long. Problems arise, since Ohio has (or had) 5 Rockvilles in as many counties, and 3 streams called Williams Creek in two other counties, but none adjacent to each other.[32]

Farmer John Robinson was driving his buggy near Phillipsburg, in early August 1883, when an 18-foot snake "of an entirely unknown species" dropped from a tree, onto the road. According to Cincinnati's *Commercial-Gazette*: "It had a monstrous flat head and darted its fangs out in a savage manner, and its eyes glowed like coals of fire." Fortunately, after several moments, it retreated.[33]

Three years later, almost to the day, a black snake 12 to 15 feet long frightened berry-pickers in Johnson's Woods, 5 miles north of Westerville.[34]

In July 1887, an engineer on the Baltimore & Ohio Railroad spotted a black "monster snake" beside the tracks near Marengo. A hunt ensued, and Dave Hunt shot the reptile 3 miles west of Sparta. It reportedly measured 17 feet, 2 inches.[35]

On April 17, 1889, while digging a well in the northwestern sector of Lorain County, a farmer named Semms or Somms unearthed two remarkable skeletons. One was that of a 19-foot snake, with ribs "the size of a small pig's" and a rattle consisting of 17 segments, the largest 6 inches

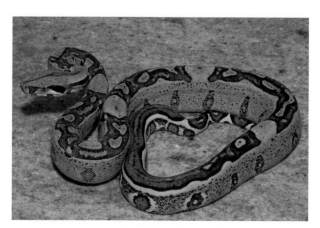

Was a tropical boa constrictor at large in 19th-century Ohio? *Credit: U.S. Fish & Wildlife Service*

in diameter. Inside that skeleton, as if swallowed, lay "the entire skeleton of a man of tremendous stature," clutching a stone ax in its right hand. Incredibly, neither relic was preserved.[36]

Five months later, Dr. F. M. Blaine was pruning hedges at his home near Great Bend, when a snake reared 6 feet off the ground and struck at him across a fence. It missed, then fled, leaving Blaine with an impression of its foul breath.[37]

On July 29, 1892, G. W. Beckett told the *Hamilton Daily Republican* that he had killed two 8-foot black snakes the previous day, at his farm in western Butler County. A larger serpent plagued the neighborhood, he said, dining on pigs and chickens. It measured 20 feet and had a head "the size of a bushel measure."[38]

One year later, on July 30, 1893, a day-long hunt failed to capture a 20-foot snake seen at Mutual, in Champaign County.[39]

On September 26, 1894, Newark's *Daily Advocate* reported the slaying of a 14-foot snake that had terrorized Liberty Township "for a long time past."[40]

In June 1895, farmers at Amanda reported losing lambs and piglets. They blamed a wolf until June 22, when one Farmer Sinkley found a huge snake in his hog pen. His gunshots missed, but hunters found and killed the reptile on June 26. The *Ohio Democrat* described it as a 31-foot anaconda, which reportedly escaped from a traveling circus in 1887. Its skin, earmarked for the Smithsonian Institute, never reached that destination.[41]

May 1896 found Summit County farmers on alert, arming against the same 12-foot snake "which caused a great sensation and much terror two years ago." L. M. Kepler saw the snake on May 24, describing it as 12 feet long and 2 feet in circumference.[42]

Days later, in June, James Starkey met an 18-foot snake at Rose Run, near Salineville. The reptile eluded hunters, as it had for "several years" past.[43]

News of that event prompted a letter from one "Rube," published in Newark's *Daily Advocate* on July 19, 1896. The author described a 20-foot snake that had frightened residents of Homer from his childhood to the present year.[44]

December 1897 brought the story of a "monster snake" from Cochranton, where sawmill workers tried to crush the reptile with logs, then saw the tree trunks hurled aside "as if they had been mere twigs."[45]

Residents of Kelleys Island, in Lake Erie, reported a giant snake prowling their 4.6-square-mile preserve in August 1898. It resembled a log, stretched across a road with its head and tail concealed in shrubbery, but length was difficult to estimate. Sandusky's *Register* was clearly in error, describing the road as "only about 600 feet wide."[46]

Summer of 1899 saw lambs disappearing from farms in Trumbull County. In late July, 4 farmers traveling near Mesopotamia surprised a "timber black snake" in the act of swallowing a calf and shot it dead. The reptile measured 12 feet, 10.5 inches long and was "as large around as an ordinary stovepipe."[47]

20th-Century Titans

In the third week of July 1901, an even larger snake was killed at Redtown. It measured 15 feet, 3 inches long.[48]

Around the same time, sightings of a monster snake occurred in Wayne County's Franklin and Wooster Townships. Hunting parties organized on August 1 and 3 failed to locate the reptile, described as "nearly as thick as a man's body and fully 25 feet in length."[49]

Trackers at Loudonville were luckier on August 7, 1901, when they killed a 20-foot snake, "supposed to have escaped from some circus."[50]

Newton Collins killed 5 snakes under a Cincinnati railroad bridge on July 10, 1903. Four were rattlers, but a local "snake expert" identified the fifth as a 9-foot boa constrictor.[51]

Newark firefighters killed another boa, 13 feet long, on August 18, 1903. Again, reporters pegged it as a fugitive from some unnamed traveling show.[52]

Kelleys Island made news again on September 27, 1904, as hunters chased, but failed to catch, a 10-foot snake "thick as a stovepipe."[53]

In early March 1906, Jerry Gump and others killed a supposed blue racer, 1 inch over 12 feet long, on the McCracken farm, east of Kirkwood.[54]

Hambden Township witnessed the next reptile panic in September 1909, sparked by an elusive black snake 15 feet long and 3 feet in diameter, said to devour calves.[55]

In July 1910, a farmer named Walters killed a large black snake at Newcomerstown. It measured 9 feet, 8 inches long, and 12 inches in circumference.[56]

August 1910 brought sightings of a larger snake, perhaps 30 feet long, from Amherst. The beast had a flat tail and was thick as a barber's pole.[57]

Fifteen years passed before the next report, from Lebanon, of a 20-foot snake at large in August 1925. Ten witnesses claimed sightings, while Oscar Bishop declared that the snake had prowled around his farm, "demoralizing" livestock, since 1908. Locals believed the reptile had escaped from a visiting circus in 1905.[58]

Fishermen Francis Bagenstose and Clifford Wilson made a surprise catch at Sandusky Bay, off Lake Erie, on July 19, 1931. Harold Madison,

a curator at the Cleveland Museum of Natural History, described their prize as a "tropical serpent," 18 feet long. Conflicting newspaper reports identified it as a boa constrictor or Indian python (*Python molurus*), but its description — dull gray, with a yellow head and "black coronet" — matched neither species.[59]

Hubert Wallace of Sterling Township reported seeing a "big" yellow-striped snake, 18 inches in circumference, in early September 1931. The *Lima News* reported that a similar reptile had frightened sawmill workers in 1924.[60]

Thirteen years later, in summer 1944, Ohio experienced its ultimate giant-snake frenzy. Clarence Mitchell of Peninsula was first to spot the serpent in mid-June, describing it as dark brown, 15 to 18 feet long, and thick as his thigh. Soon afterward, Roy Vaughn's wife saw the snake swallow one of her chickens, then "jump" a 4-foot fence to escape. Armed posses led by police stalked the creature — dubbed the "Peninsula Python" and "Sarah the Snake" — but all in vain. Bernard Crozier of Dresden

An Indian python was caught on Kelleys Island in July 1931.
Credit: U.S. Fish & Wildlife Service

retroactively claimed a 1941 sighting, unreported at the time, of a snake with a head "as big as a horse's, and a great round body." Peninsula mayor John Hitch declared a state of emergency, branding the snake "a menace to the peace and order, health and welfare, and generally good reputation for veracity and sobriety of our citizens." Meanwhile, the Gale brothers—Albert and George—saw a similar reptile swimming in a creek outside Cleveland. Local searches proved fruitless, but the scare is memorialized in occasional Python Day celebrations, the most recent celebrated in July 2011.[61]

Two years after those events, in July 1946, berry-picker "Clarence McC." killed a 14-foot "blacksnake" on Charles Babb's farm, 7 miles west of Zanesville. Newark's *Advocate* described it as "the longest snake of any kind seen in that vicinity in a long time."[62]

Our last case, sadly undated, comes from Tom Rumer's history of Hardin County's Scioto Marsh, published in 1999. Once a vast swamp, drained in the 1880s for the benefit of onion growers, the region is known for its tales of giant snakes. Farmer Larry Risner told Rumer of an occasion when his—Risner's—father ran over a "very large" snake with a tractor and disc harrow, which failed to kill it. Rumer notes that "assumptions about the presence of a large pythonlike snake persisted for several years."[63]

Indeed, an Internet blogger calling himself "Tecumseh" claims to have interviewed a local resident in spring 2001, recording an encounter with a giant snake that the witness and his brothers saw while fishing in the Scioto River. The anonymous informant estimated that the snake was 40 feet long and 3 feet in diameter.[64]

Officially, the largest snake on Earth is the reticulated python, with a record length of 22.8 feet listed for a captive specimen in Indonesia. While reports of much larger pythons and anacondas persist, no one has yet collected the Wildlife Conservation Society's standing offer of $50,000 for a live, healthy snake of any species measuring 30 feet or longer.[65]

Chapter 5

Unidentified

Swimming

Objects

The study of lake monsters, dubbed dracontology, is a significant part of cryptozoology. Ohio — with 2,500 lakes exceeding 2 acres and 187 larger than 10 acres, plus 4,113 rivers and streams — seems a likely place to seek aquatic cryptids.[1] And such, in fact, is the case.

Native Americans were familiar with Ohio's lake monsters long before the first white settlers arrived. Swiss-American ethnologist Albert Gatschet chronicled aboriginal legends in 1899, listing among Ohio's strange lake-dwellers a merbeing called Mänsanzhi by Miami tribesmen; a monster known to the Shawnee as Wewiwilemitá manetú or Msí kinépikwa ("great reptile"); and the Yenrish ("lion"), said by Huron-Wyandot elders to live at the bottom of Lake Erie.[2]

Gatschet, as we now find, didn't know the half of it.

Giant Catfish

Catfish (order *Siluriformes*) inhabit every continent on Earth except Antarctica. They range in size from the tiny parasitic candiru (*Vandellia cirrhosa*) of South America to Asia's Mekong giant catfish (*Pangasianodon gigas*) that exceeds 10 feet in length, and Eurasia's wels catfish (*Silurus glanis*) with a record length of 9 feet, 7 inches. North America's largest known species, the blue catfish (*Ictalurus furcatus*), boasts a record weight of 143 pounds, for a specimen caught in Virginia on June 18, 2011. Prior to that, a 104-pound blue held the record, pulled from the Ohio River in 1999. The longest blue catfish on record, caught in Missouri in 2010, measured 4 feet, 9 inches long.[3]

Those records pale, however, beside reports of truly giant catfish in Ohio waters. Ronan Coghlan alludes to a dead catfish found in the Ohio River that measured 25 feet, but he unfortunately cites no source. Author Ron Schaffner offers vague tales of undewater welders who refused to work on Ohio River bridges after sighting giant catfish. Various locks and dams on the Ohio also have a reputation as the lairs of huge, man-eating catfish.[4]

True or false? Do huge native catfish exist in Ohio, or have giant foreign species invaded U.S. waterways like other exotics including the common carp (*Cyprinus carpio*), walking catfish (*Clarias batrachus*), snakeheads (family *Channidae*), and others? Until a true giant is caught, the question remains unanswered.

Indescribable

On January 30, 1959, a truck driver traveling along U.S. Route 52, west of New Richmond, saw a bizarre creature emerge from the Ohio River. It was, he said, so ugly that he "couldn't begin to describe it." Two hours later, a witness in Covington, Kentucky, reported sighting a beast she thought was an octopus, where the Licking River empties into the Ohio. It was gray, "with a lopsided chest, ugly tentacles, and rolls of fat running horizontally around a bald head."[5]

All known species of octopus (order *Octopoda*) live in salt water, but specimens have been found in or near the Ohio River on two occasions. Both were discovered at Falls of the Ohio State Park, at Clarksville, Indiana. One was found ashore in 1999; the second, with a 6-foot arm spread, was hooked by an angler on August 7, 2006. In the second case, a Kentucky film student admitted placing the octopus in the Ohio as part of a school project.[6]

Release the Kraken!

If local tales are true, a larger cephalopod may dwell in Williams County's Nettle Lake, sprawling over 115 acres, with a maximum recorded depth of 27 feet. Wildlife authorities count 21 species of fish inhabiting Nettle Lake, but their list does not include a monster known to locals as the "kraken."[7]

An early depiction of the kraken. *Credit: Author's collection*

Historically, the kraken is a huge sea monster, said to grasp and sink ships with its many arms. Most modern ichthyologists believe those legends sprang from sightings of a giant squid (genus *Architeuthis*) or a colossal squid (*Mesonychoteuthis hamiltoni*), both deep-sea species rarely seen.[8] But what, if anything, lurks in Nettle Lake?

Unfortunately, tales are vague, dating from 1941 with hearsay anecdotes of "a monstrous, bottom-dwelling creature" dragging swimmers and boaters underwater to their doom. Even that sparse information is enough to prompt local "Days of the Kraken" celebrations complete with parades, barbecues, and sales of local handicrafts.[9] As for the monster, it appears to be retired.

Nettle Lake, scene of alleged "kraken" attacks.
Credit: U.S. Geological Survey

Slaven's Pond

Sometime in 1953, Joe Roush saw an unidentified creature 6 to 8 feet long swimming in Slaven's Pond, at Bainbridge. *Fate* magazine covered the incident in March 1954, describing the beast as a "sea serpent," but no further information is presently available. Ohio has two towns called Bainbridge, widely separated from each other in Geauga and Ross Counties.[10] Oddly, my inquiries to local officials and historians elicited denials that any such body of water exists in either county.

Rush Creek

Ronan Coghlan offers us an undated case, involving "an unidentified monster at Rush Creek (Ohio), which hounds refused to follow. It left clawmarks, but was never actually seen." It is not clear from that account whether the creature was aquatic or terrestrial, and Coghlan's source—Rich La Monica's Norka of Akron—no longer exists online.[11]

Our problem is compounded by a multitude of Rush Creeks in Ohio. Streams called Rush Creek exist in Fairfield, Marion, and Shelby Counties. Fairfield and Logan Counties each have townships named Rush Creek. And finally, 300-acre Rush Creek Lake spans the line between Fairfield and Perry Counties.[12] Without more detailed information, clarification is impossible.

The Olentangy River

On April 4, 1982, Columbus police logged a report of a hippopotamus swimming in the Olentangy River, near West North Broadway. The first officer on scene confirmed that identification, while a bystander thought the paddling beast was a cougar. Firefighters soon arrived, Battalion Chief Gene Wedemeyer telling reporters that the animal "wasn't as big as a seal. We thought it might be an otter."[13]

North American river otters (*Lontra canadensis*) inhabit most of the continent, but were considered to be extirpated from Ohio by the early 1900s. Four years after the Olentangy River incident, the state's Division of Wildlife reintroduced otters in the Grand River, Killbuck Creek, Little Muskingum River, and Stillwater Creek. Since then, they have been seen in

nearly two-thirds of Ohio's 88 counties.[14] It is unclear how any sober person could mistake an otter—with a record length of 42 inches and a top weight of 30-odd pounds—for the world's fourth-largest terrestrial mammal.

Ohio's Olentangy River.
Credit: U.S. Geological Survey

Witnesses reported a hippopotamus swimming in the Olentangy.
Credit: U.S. Fish & Wildlife Service

An otter is not easily confused with a hippo.
Credit: U.S. Fish & Wildlife Service

Charles Mill Lake

This reservoir, covering 1,350 acres in Ashland and Richland Counties, was created with construction of the Charles Mill Dam on the Black Fork of the Mohican River, in 1935. Its strange tale— reported by teenagers Wayne Armstrong, Michael Lane, and Dennis Patterson a quarter-century later—bears no resemblance to "normal" lake monster reports.[15]

The 3 youths were killing time on the lakeshore near Ruggles, on the night of March 28, 1959, when a 7-foot humanoid creature rose out of the water. The boys described its luminous green eyes and large webbed feet, while claiming that it had no arms. Police responding to the call allegedly found tracks on the shoreline resembling imprints from a scuba diver's fins. Loren Coleman credits the beast with a second appearance in 1963, while other researchers link that sighting to Bigfoot (see Chapter 7).[16] In either case, no further stories have emerged from the vicinity within the past half-century.

South Bay Bessie

Lake Erie, with a surface area of 9,940 square miles and a maximum recorded depth of 210 feet, is the fourth largest of the Great Lakes and the tenth largest lake on Earth. Ohio shares its 850-mile shoreline with Michigan, Pennsylvania, New York, and the Canadian province of Ontario.[17] It also shares a monster whose appearances have startled witnesses for some 220 years.

Tales of the creature begin with Seneca tribesmen, who spoke of "a huge water serpent that lived in the Niagara River and Lake Erie." The first sighting by whites occurred in 1793, when the captain of the sloop *Felicity* met a serpentine creature "more than a rod [16.5 feet] in length." Lake Erie does harbor a subspecies of northern water snake (*Nerodia sipedon insularum*), but its record length is 4 feet, 7 inches.[18]

The monster surfaced twice in 1817. First, on July 7, Captain Shubael West and his crew aboard the schooner *Delia* saw a "serpent" 30 to 40 feet long, 5 miles offshore. Later, another boat's crew fired muskets at a copper-colored monster 60 feet in length, to no effect.[19]

In 1887, while fishing near Toledo, two brothers named Dusseau saw a creature 20 to 30 feet long writhing on shore, presumably in its death throes. They compared it to sturgeon, but with "arms." The brothers left to get rope and secure their prize, but returned to find it gone, no trace remaining except silver scales the size of dollar coins.[20]

In July 1892, Captain Woods of the schooner *Madaline* met "a huge serpent" while en route from Buffalo, New York, to Toledo. The beast seemed to be "wrestling about in the waters, as if fighting with an unseen foe," its eyes "viciously sparkling." Woods and his crew pegged its length at 50 feet, with a 4-foot circumference, further noting its prominent fins.[21]

On May 5, 1896, the monster cavorted off Crystal Beach, near Fort Erie, in plain view of 4 witnesses. Observing the 30-foot beast for 45 minutes, they offered clear descriptions of its dog-like head and pointed tail.[22]

On July 8, 1898, the *Sandusky Daily Register* reported that Lake Erie's monster population had been "verified and their existence can no longer be questioned." Described as "fierce, ugly, coiling creatures" 25 to 30 feet long, the beasts were said to be amphibious.[23]

The first known monster hoax at Lake Erie occurred on April Fool's Day 1912, when the *Sandusky Daily Register* described a "sea monster" smashing its way through a sheet of ice near Kelleys Island, churning toward shore with mouth agape and fangs displayed.[24]

Nineteen years later, in July 1931, it briefly seemed as if one of the creatures had been captured at Sandusky. That specimen proved to be a python (see Chapter 4), but the affinity of serpentine cryptids for Sandusky Bay prompted Ohioans to dub their monster "South Bay Bessie"—or simply "Bessie," imitating "Nessie" of Scotland's Loch Ness.[25]

Ken Golic logged the next sighting in 1960, while night-fishing from a Sandusky pier. The creature was "cigar-shaped," its back rising 12 to 18 inches above water.[26]

In 1969, while fishing off South Bass Island in western Lake Erie, Jim Schindler saw Bessie pass within 6 feet of him. He could not estimate the beast's length, but pegged its width at 2 feet.[27]

Theresa Kovach of Akron saw Bessie from the Cedar Point Causeway in September 1981, describing a serpentine creature that "was so large that it could easily capsize a boat. It seemed to be playing."[28]

In 1983, Mary Landoll reported a dawn sighting off Huron's Rye Beach. She first mistook the creature for a capsized boat 40 to 50 feet long, then saw a long neck raised, revealing an eye and "a grin going up one side" of its face. Again, Bessie seemed to be playing.[29]

Tony Schill of Avon was boating with several friends in summer 1985, offshore from Vermilion, when they saw a dark brown "serpent" with a flat tail, showing 5 "humps" on the lake's surface. "No way it was a sturgeon," Schill insisted. Later in the same year, Dale Munro watched Bessie for 3 or 4 minutes, near the Lorain Coast Guard Station. It was twice the length of his 16-foot boat, with 3 black humps visible.[30]

Four years later, in May or June 1989, Gail Kasner procured a fishfinder printout from boat owner Ken Smith of Streetsboro. The graph appears to show a 35-foot object maneuvering at a depth of 30 feet.[31]

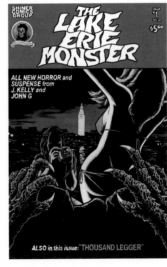

Kelleys Island, scene of a 1912 "sea monster" hoax
and a 1991 "Bessie" videotaping.
Credit: U.S. Geological Survey

A tabloid newspaper's treatment of South Bay Bessie.
Credit: Author's collection

A fanciful comic book send-up of Bessie.
Credit: Author's collection

In July 8, 1990, Susan Seeson of Salem saw a creature matching Bessie's description two miles offshore from Cedar Point, a Sandusky amusement park.[32]

September 1990 brought a rash of monster sightings. Florida tourist Bob Soracco, jet-skiing near Port Clinton on September 3, saw something he took for a porpoise, showing gray-spotted humps above water. "It was very long as I moved closer and it was going down," he said. The next day, Harold Bricker called DNR rangers at East Harbor State Park, reporting that a 35-foot creature had passed within 1,000 feet of his boat as he and his family fished off Cedar Point. Huron fire inspectors Steve Dircks and Jim Johnson saw Bessie on September 11, from a third-story window facing the lake. It was dark blue or black, 30 to 45 feet long, revealing 3 humps that were "flat on top." During the week of September 16, fisherman Dennis Szececinski saw a long black creature swimming near Toledo's water intake structure, 3 miles offshore in Maumee Bay.[33]

Monster fever gripped Huron and environs. Limnologist/ oceanographer Charles Herdendorf proposed a scientific name for Bessie: *Obscura eriensis huronii* ("rarely-seen Lake Erie monster indigenous to Huron waters"). City officials proclaimed Huron the "National Live Capture and Control Center for the Lake Erie Monster," requested a "monster-hunting" permit from the DNR, and built a holding pen labeled "Future Home of the Lake Erie Monster." Tom Solberg, owner of the Huron Lagoons Marina, raised a reward for Bessie's capture, worth $102,700 in cash and prizes, supplemented from a Lloyd's of London insurance policy that cost local merchants $5,000 per year.[34]

All in vain.

In July 1991, while vacationing on Kelleys Island, George Repicz videotaped 20 seconds of some unknown object moving offshore. His companions could "barely see" the thing caught by Repicz's zoom lens, and skeptics dismissed it as a floating log.[35]

Huron resident Thomas Schofield built a 35-foot plastic-and-plywood replica of Bessie in 1994, securing it near the Huron River's mouth with a 300-foot leash, where it bobbed serenely until 2004, disappearing around the time of Schofield's death. His sons replaced it on Father's Day 2005, with a Styrofoam model 27 feet long and 4 feet high, complete with glowing eyes and a 13-foot "baby monster" companion.[36]

Bessie's next live appearance occurred on July 28, 1998, when South Carolina tourist Leslee Rasgaitis and several relatives watched a black 3-humped object passing 500 feet offshore from Huntington Beach at Bay Village.[37]

Around the same time, "young Earth" creationist Carl Baugh began to display the "Erie Baby," a supposed juvenile lake monster, at his Creation Evidence Museum in Glen Rose, Texas. According to Baugh, Cleveland

Boat wakes like this one, photographed at South Bay, may explain some surface sightings.
Credit: Author's collection

A model of South Bay Bessie.
Credit: Author's collection

taxidermist Larry "Pete" Petersen found the 3-foot carcass beached sometime in 1992 and preserved it as an attraction for his suburban bait shop. Baugh bought the object for his museum, while fellow religionist Kent "Dr. Dino" Hovind — presently serving a 10-year federal prison term for tax fraud — promoted the creature in seminars as proof of creationism.[38] According to Hovind, it is a:

> strange looking little fellow. Four flippers and has a tail sort of like a fish. He [Baugh] said it had something like pouches on the side of its cheeks....They've done a DNA analysis and a CAT scan x-ray. It had a fish hook stuck up in its head. Apparently somebody caught it sometime in the past and broke the line. The fish hook is still in there, it shows up on the CAT scan. Strange little critter.[39]

Researcher Glen Kuban contacted Peterson, discovering that he believed the creature was "some kind of fish," badly decayed and mauled by hungry seagulls. He then "decided to stuff it and fashion it into a sea-serpent like creature as an attention-getting display for an upcoming taxidermy trade show," notching the long fin on its back to "make it appear more dragon like." Peterson considered it a "joke," while Kuban speculated that the animal might be a common burbot or eelpout (*Lota lota*). Carl Baugh continued to promote the creature as a "throwback" or an "exotic unclassified eel."[40]

Despite that hoax, Bessie has a firm grip on pop culture. Cleveland resident Daniel Gilbert, founder-president of Quicken Loans, purchased the defunct Utah Grizzlies hockey team in May 2006 and revived it in January 2007 as the Lake Erie Monsters, named in Bessie's honor. The Great Lakes Brewing Company manufactures a seasonal ale called Lake Erie Monster, and a popular rock band called South Bay Bessie operates from headquarters in Flint, Michigan.[41]

Bessie's legend took a sinister turn in August 2001, when Brenda McCormack and two other residents of Port Dover, Ontario, suffered painful bites while swimming in Lake Erie's shallows. None of the victims saw their attacker, but Dr. Harold Hynscht, who treated all 3, officially "ruled out piranhas, lamprey eels, snapping turtles and walleye, goby and muskellunge fish." The predator, said Dr. Hynscht, was "a big honking fish," perhaps a bowfin (*Amia calva*), but he could

Logo of the Lake Erie Monsters hockey team. *Credit: Author's collection*

An advertisement for Lake Erie Monster ale. *Credit: Author's collection*

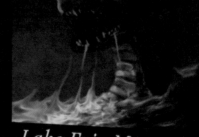

not be certain. "One of the consistent elements of the stories I've heard is that it happened so fast they hardly had time to react," Hynscht said. "Whatever is doing this is doing so because of territory. It's not doing this because it's hungry."[42]

In fact, the muskellunge or musky (*Esox masquinongy*) is an ambush predator that may reach 6 feet in length. It is related to the northern pike (*E. lucius*), another vicious species with a record 5-foot length, that interbreeds with muskies to produce a "tiger muskellunge" whose males are sterile. No exotic snakeheads are confirmed as living in Lake Erie, but a fisherman hooked one at Burnham Harbor, on Lake Michigan, in October 2004.[43]

Officially, Lake Erie's largest native fish is the lake sturgeon (*Acipenser fulvescens*), a primitive species that may live more than 150 years, only reaching sexual maturity in its third decade of life. The world record lake sturgeon, pulled from Lake Erie by a New York fisherman in summer 1998, measured 7 feet, 4 inches and tipped the scales at 250 pounds. Eurasian species reportedly exceed 18 feet and boast a record weight of 4,400 pounds.[44]

Sturgeons have been proposed as Bessie candidates by various authorities, including Ohio Division of Wildlife fisheries biologist David Davies. Once so abundant in Lake Erie that their bodies were burned as steamship fuel, sturgeons were nearly extirpated by the early 1900s, then made a comeback in the 1990s, with 20 to 30 spotted each year by game wardens. Now protected by law, they must be released if hooked—as angler Frank McDonald did with a 3-foot specimen caught in August 2006.[45]

But does any known fish species truly solve the mystery of South Bay Bessie? Or do the reports spanning 220 years suggest that Lake Erie may harbor ... something else?

Port Dover, Ontario, scene of attacks by an unidentified aquatic predator in 2001.
Credit: U.S. Geological Survey

One potential Port Dover suspect, the muskellunge.
Credit: U.S. Fish & Wildlife Service

Could Bessie be a giant sturgeon?
Credit: U.S. Fish & Wildlife Service

Chapter 6

Haunted

Skies

Ohio skies teem with wildlife. Official sources recognize 247 native bird species and 11 species of bats competing for air space and food in the Buckeye State. The largest species, in descending order of size, are the golden eagle (*Aquila chrysaetos*), with a record wingspan of 9 feet, 2 inches; the bald eagle (*Haliaeetus leucocephalus*), with a top wingspan of 8 feet; the turkey vulture (*Cathartes aura*), with a record 6-foot wingspan; the great horned owl (*Bubo virginianus*), top wingspan 5 feet; and the red-tailed hawk (*Buteo jamaicensis*), with a record wingspan of 4 feet, 9 inches.[1]

By this point in our journey, it should come as no surprise that much larger—and stranger—creatures have been spotted in Ohio's air space.

The golden eagle is Ohio's largest recognized bird species.
Credit: U.S. Fish & Wildlife Service

Big Birds

Native Americans from coast to coast recognized the existence of huge raptors, generically called "thunderbirds," that preyed on animals including deer and human beings. Sightings of truly giant birds continue to the present day, from widely separated areas of the United States and Canada. Ohio has logged fewer modern sightings than nearby Pennsylvania (see *Strange Pennsylvania Monsters*, 2012), but the available reports are striking.

On November 26, 1966, Marvin Shock and 3 companions spent two hours watching a quartet of thunderbirds at Cat's Creek, in Lowell. At rest on tree limbs, the birds "looked about as big as a man," 4 to 5 feet tall, with beaks 5 to 6 inches long, and a 10-foot wingspan in flight. Their backs were dark brown, their breasts gray, and each had a "reddish cast" to its head.[2]

Eight days later, on December 4, 5 pilots saw a larger bird soaring over Gallia-Meigs Regional Airport in Gallipolis. At first, they mistook it for an airplane, gliding at an altitude of some 300 feet, at 70 miles per hour. The creature soared overhead without flapping its wings. Witness Everett Wedge grabbed a camera and rushed to his plane, intending to pursue the bird, but it had vanished by the time he got airborne.[3]

The nearest thing to thunderbirds that science recognizes are the prehistoric teratorns (family *Teratornithidae*), known from fossil remains found in North and South America. The largest species, *Argentavis magnificens*, boasted a wingspan of 23 feet. One North American species, *Teratornis merriami*, had a 12.5-foot wingspan, while another—*Aiolornis incredibilis*, known only from beak and wing-bone fragments—was 40 percent larger than *T. merriami*. All teratorns are presumed extinct for at least 10,000 years, but some cryptozoologists speculate that survivors may account for modern thunderbird reports.[4]

Urban Legend?

Ronan Coghlan reports that, in 1893, two women navigating Cincinnati's streets by buggy reported seeing a winged creature with a wicked beak and clawed feet. That might include any large raptor, but Fortean author W. R. Benedict suggests that it may have been a griffin—a composite beast from classical mythology that bore an eagle's head and wings, with a lion's limbs and body. No other sightings of the creature were recorded.[5]

A sculpted model of an ancient teratorn.
Credit: Author's collection

Calling Batman!

Coghlan relates another tale, this one from Akron, occurring sometime during 1960. Two witnesses allegedly saw a large bipedal creature with bat-like wings, walking "with apparent unconcern" along an unnamed road. Coghlan adds that "various rumors" describe similar creatures dwelling in a nearby region called The Gorge. His source ("Ohio Cryptids — Winged Things") proved untraceable, but 155-acre Gorge Metro Park is a well-known attraction in Akron.[6]

Mothman

Ohio's 1966 T-bird sightings occurred in conjunction with appearances of a mysterious man-sized flying creature, popularly known as "Mothman," in neighboring West Virginia. That entity was first reported from Clendinin in 1965, and while it spent most of its time around Point Pleasant — where a statue of it stands today — it was not physically restricted to the Mountain State.[7]

On November 17, 1966, a teenager driving on State Route 7 near Cheshire reported being chased by something that matched Mothman's description: "a gray man-shaped creature" with glowing red eyes and a 10-foot wingspan.[8]

Three weeks later, on December 7, 4 Nelsonville women traveling along U.S. Route 33 near Gallipolis — scene of the big bird sighting 4 days earlier — reported a near-collision with "a brownish silver man-shaped flying creature with glowing red eyes."[9]

Contrary to popular belief, Ohio sightings of creatures resembling Mothman did not end in the 1960s. Ronan Coghlan reports that a similar creature — gray and prone to shrieking — attacked unidentified persons in woods near Columbus, during 2003. Coghlan's online source (www.mothmanlives.com) was shut down for "revamping" throughout my research for this volume, leaving further details unavailable.[10]

Writing in 2005, from the source sited above, Coghlan adds the undated case of a white or gray bipedal creature, man-sized, glimpsed by an unnamed Ohio driver at some undisclosed location. According to Coghlan, the witness "was inclined to compare [it] with a Mothman, but he discerned no wings."[11]

A statue of Mothman in Point Pleasant, West Virginia.
Credit: Author's collection

In November 2008, a Monroe County resident driving home from work, at 4 a.m., saw a "large creature crouched down on the ground with bright red, glowing eyes that looked directly at him." It "had very large wings which were also kind of wrapped around it as it crouched in the middle of the road." He swerved around it, then checked his rearview mirror and found that it had vanished.[12]

On September 14, 2009, a motorist observed a "solid black entity" standing beside Hudson Drive in the city of Stow. It was 9 or 10 feet tall, with "no discernible head or facial features." The witness did not mention wings, but later drew a sketch for the Munroe Falls Paranormal Society that resembled West Virginia's creature from 40 years past.[13]

On January 29, 2011, Cincinnati witness "Liz" saw Mothman while driving home from a date. Clearly visible under a neighbor's outdoor lights, it was a "massive thing" as tall as the doors of a nearby shed, with "two curved-like masses coming from the sides" and "deep red, glowing eyes." Liz sent an instant message to friend "Allie," who subsequently heard a light tapping at her bedroom window. Opening the blinds, she "could faintly see something red and glowing, like taillights, that had somehow made their way into the neighbor's backyard." In retrospect, Allie was "not sure what this was; a frightening delusion or a real situation."[14]

March 10, 2011, brought another report, this one from Sciotodale. Returning from a store, witness "Veronica" and a friend saw a creature gliding with "no wing motion," some 80 feet above their heads. It was tan in color, had a wingspan of 12 to 15 feet, and appeared to be traveling around 20 miles per hour.[15]

While some researchers speculate that Mothman might be an extraterrestrial or a visitor from another dimension, author Mark Hall offers a more mundane explanation. Simply stated, he believes the creature may be an unclassified species of giant owl that he calls "Bighoot," known to Ohio's aboriginal Wyandot people as the "Flying Head."[16]

Author William Connelly, writing in 1899, reported that "[t]he Flying Heads plagued the Wyandots. They were more dangerous and troublesome during rainy, foggy, or misty weather. They could enter a cloud of fog, or mist, or rime, and in it approach a Wyandot village unseen. They were cruel and wicked hooh-kehs and cannibals. They caused sickness; they were vampires, and lay in wait for people, whom they caught and devoured. They carried away children; they blighted the tobacco and other crops; they stole and devoured the game after the hunter had killed it. Fire was the most potent agency with which to resist them. The lightning sometimes killed one."[17]

Hall reports what he believes to be a modern Bighoot sighting from Ohio's Highland County, in August 1982. According to the eyewitness report:

> while fishing in Rocky Fork Lake...we drifted into a pristine cove on the southwest side and noted with utter disbelief an old tall topless tree trunk approximately 9-10 feet high, 12 inches around, move about 4 feet sideways. (This was on shore about 20 feet inland among like-looking trees and underbrush.) Again it moved, only this time there was a partial twisting or rotation from the top 18-24 inches. It slowly maneuvered backward (keeping erect like a tree) into the woods, with NO NOISES from it or the underbrush, as graceful as a bird thru [sic] a tree. It stopped in the middle of a sunlight clearing...[18]

Seconds later, the creature's "wings unfolded with a span greater than most small airplanes." It soon returned to its "tree appearance," but continued watching the witness with a "semblance of two eyes" as her boat moved away. "One year later, same lake, and a half mile or so from that first cove, this figure appeared near [the] shoreline again. (It seemed taller or leaner.) This time [I] got a look at its legs and feet — yellowish grainy like chicken legs....They were so thin and short for its height. Three long slender toes with a hooked toe or nail on the lower leg. (I won't swear to toes being 3 or 4.)"[19]

The great horned owl — mistaken for Mothman? Credit: U.S. Fish & Wildlife Service

The aforementioned great horned owl is North America's largest known species, while Blakiston's fish owl (*Bubo blakistoni*) and the Eurasian eagle-owl (*B. bubo*) vie for honors as Earth's largest, with record wingspans of 6 feet, 9 inches and 6 feet, 2 inches, respectively. The prehistoric Cuban giant owl (*Ornimegalonyx*) stood 3 feet, 7 inches tall, but was a flightless species, presumed extinct for some 10,000 years.[20]

On Leather Wings

Much older than the teratorns or *Ornimegalonyx* were the pterosaurs, winged reptiles of Triassic and Cretaceous Periods (210 to 65.5 million years ago). Science presently recognizes 179 genera of pterosaurs, including the largest known flying animals. The largest complete fossil specimen of *Quetzalcoatlus* had a wingspan of 52.2 feet, while estimates for *Hatzegopteryx* (though never found complete, so far) range from 39 to 65 feet.[21]

Most archaeologists agree that pterosaurs became extinct some 65.3 million years before the first *Homo sapiens* appeared on Earth—but sightings of creatures strongly resembling prehistoric fliers continue to the present day, with some reported from Ohio.

In summer 1967, James Morgan and 4 other witnesses saw an animal "resembling a pterodactyl" fly past their homes outside Middletown. It was dark in color, seemed to have no feathers, and glided on wings 15 to 20 feet across.[22]

One night in 1991, several young men were exploring an abandoned barn near Middletown, when they discovered a bird-like creature, some 6 feet, 4 inches tall, with leathery skin in place of feathers. It watched them for a moment, then took wing, frightening the youths so badly that they fled on foot, leaving their bicycles behind.[23]

In summer 2003, a young man from Antwerp reportedly saw a long-tailed pterosaur fly over the Maumee River, near the bridge for State Route 49. He described it as "huge...about a 4.5-foot tail, 10 feet from head to end of tail. Long skinny tail with a spade." The following year, during "the hottest time of the summer," he saw the same beast or its twin near the same location.[24]

Witness "Jan" from Antwerp supported that account with her own undated sighting, telling author Jonathan Whitcomb, "I have seen the same thing. It was huge. And it matches your description. About 4.5 feet tall, 10 feet from head to end of tail. Long skinny tail with a spade about 3 to 4-inches from end of tail. It had a wing span of I would say 8 to 10 feet. Dark green skin, sort of like an alligator. It had round long pointed teeth."[25]

On October 9, 2005, while driving to his church for Sunday services, a minister in Mount Vernon "happened to notice a creature in the sky." Slowing his car for a better look, he observed that "it appeared to have no feathers. It was a leathery, grayish color. The beak seemed to protrude from its face, not like a separate part of the head, but looking to be the same color, etc. Its wings did not look like bird wings, but also appeared leathery and bat-like (I have seen actual bats in caves and zoos). The kicker, for me, was the tail: longer than most bird tails I am used to, no feathers, and with a diamond-shaped point at the end. I am not very good at judging the size of animals in the air. I will say this, he was high up and yet I could tell everything about him/her that I told you. Easily larger than a bald eagle."[26]

A reconstructed skeleton of *Quetzalcoatlus,* largest known flying creature from Earth's prehistory. *Credit: Author's collection*

Long tails were generally found among early, smaller pterosaurs (suborder *Rhamphorhynchoidea*), while tails diminished in later, larger species to the point of near-invisibility. Rhamphorhynchoids are presumed to have become extinct around 124.5 million years ago, making an appearance in the 21st century all the more unlikely.[27]

Finally, a motorist driving near Kenton, on State Route 309, describes an incident occurring on June 26, 2010. "I had a creature swoop down and glide over my hood of my car," she told Whitcomb. "It glided smoothly and looked like a Pterodactyl, and I thought to myself, 'What the ....' as it smoothly flew into a thick area of trees....I could see almost the bones in its wings but I did NOT see feathers at all."[28]

And Something Else ...

Ronan Coghlan offers our last case of unknown flying creatures from Ohio, sadly without much detail. His account reads, in full:

> Triangular creatures, apparently alive, with flapping wings, were seen over Norton Acres (Ohio) in 1980. The witness at first took them for kites.[29]

Norton Acres is a subdivision of Norton, a city straddling the Summit-Wayne County line. Unfortunately, Coghlan's source (www.cryptozoo.com) no longer exists. And there the story ends, as it began — in mystery.

Chapter 7

On Bigfoot's Trail

iscussions of Bigfoot/Sasquatch normally focus on the Pacific Northwest, but reports have been filed from 49 of the United States (excluding Hawaii) and every Canadian province. Ohio witnesses meet hairy bipeds frequently—often enough, in fact, to keep at least 6 groups conducting field investigations, while the Buckeye Bigfoot rates a special Facebook page.[1]

Delaware tribesmen greeted 18th-century settlers with tales of shaggy forest-dwellers who accepted offerings of food "to keep the peace," but Ohio's first white sighting came 4 years after the Civil War. No two sources agree on the total number of Sasquatch reports, footprint discoveries, and similar incidents logged from Ohio, but comparison of published works and sightings logged online reveal 516 distinct accounts recorded between 1869 and 2012, with several more vaguely describing multiple encounters.

Hollywood plays Bigfoot for low-budget frights.
Credit: Author's collection

The 19th Century

On January 23, 1869, the Mankato (Minnesota) *Weekly Record* reported a hairy "wild man...gigantic in height," prowling around Gallipolis. It had attacked a carriage, mauling the driver with murderous "and savage intensity," until his daughter hurled a rock and frightened it away.[2]

Another wild man, "covered with hair and looking like a bear," frightened hunters Bob Bradley and Henry Raush near New Lisbon (now simply Lisbon), in early December 1883. Both men fired shots, apparently wounding the creature, then dropped their empty guns and fled.[3]

Holmes County hunters met "a wild man, or some other strange being" in November 1886. It escaped by diving into Killbuck Creek, leaving pursuers to surmise that it was "no relative of the famous wild man or Rockaway."[4]

Belmont County farmers organized to hunt a livestock-killing predator in August 1891. Witness Samuel Crow described the thing as 5 feet tall when standing erect, able to "walk and run as well on 2 as 4 legs." It was "covered with dark reddish hair, has two large ears, small eyes, teeth like a wild boar, huge hands and paws." Despite the dragnet, it escaped.[5]

A "gorillalike object" attacked timber-cutters Bob Forner and Charles Lukins near Rome on May 26, 1897. They escaped, convinced that it was "undoubtedly the same [creature] seen a number of times several weeks ago."[6]

That same month, at Logan, farmers searched in vain for a "strange animal" that shrieked at night, while snatching sheep and lambs.[7]

The 20th Century

1901-1959

On August 1, 1901, the *Lima Times Democrat* reported a "wildman" terrorizing berry-pickers around "Bereau" — presumably Berea. Posses searched in vain for the offender.[8]

A "strange being, apparently half man and half beast," harassed residents of Beaverdam and Rockport during April 1902, but a reference to the hairy biped being "scantily clad" in "dress peculiar to one of the male sex" may suggest a crazed hermit.[9]

No clothes adorned the shaggy beast "as big as Goliath" that prowled around New Philadelphia in October 1904. Hunters nearly cornered it on October 10, but it proved "fleet as the wind and lithe as the deer," outrunning their fastest hounds.[10]

Sometime in 1912, a woman and her son met a "monster" on their farm, 10 miles outside Gallipolis. It had "a bulky head, appeared to have no neck to it, and monstrous wide shoulders; probably twice as wide as a man's shoulders." It followed them for some distance, then vanished in the woods.[11]

A strange, confusing tale emerged from Walhonding in July 1919. First reports described a "full grown ape" at large, supposedly a fugitive from "a Cleveland zoo," with a $2,000 reward offered for its capture. Three witnesses were named, but one of them—Rev. C.H. Hood—denied the sighting, claiming he had only seen "a large groundhog." Witnesses John Branfield and R.B. Gauley stood by their stories, with Gauley (Hood's partner in an insurance firm) disputing Hood's denial. By August 2, Hood was "undecided" as to what he saw. The bounty went unclaimed.[12]

A year later, in July 1920, "a large specimen of the African ape" appeared at Gravel Bank, 8 miles south of Marietta. Several witnesses fired at the beast, but it escaped through the trees, swinging from branch to branch.[13]

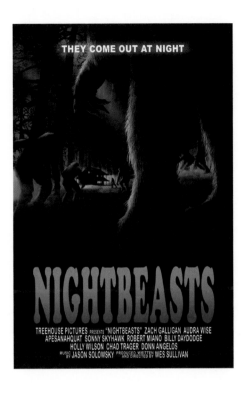

In fiction and film, Bigfoot's reputation suffers.
Credit: Author's collection

On June 6, 1930, multiple witnesses saw a "large ape" roaming free around Norwalk's Memorial Hospital. Police searched in vain for the creature, though farmer Carl Landoll found tracks of a "big anthropoid." The beast turned up in Rice Township on June 11, and was last seen at Alger on June 27. By then, reporters claimed it was "supposed to have escaped from a circus at Carey."[14]

Another unnamed circus was blamed for the "ape scare" at Chandlersville, in August 1932, while the *Coshocton Tribune* initially blamed hoaxers for ape sightings at nearby Roscoe the following month. Farmers Glenn Adams and Homer Goodin disputed that claim, with reports of separate sightings. The beast tore down fences and appeared to have a broken chain around its neck. It reached Steubenville (Jefferson County) by September 22, and thereafter vanished.[15]

A final sighting from the early 1930s was reported years after the fact by George Johnson of Sciotoville. While vague on dates, he described the beast as "very muscular," 8 feet tall, and weighing about 700 pounds.[16]

Ohio researcher Don Keating cites an interview with an unnamed witness who saw Bigfoot peering through his kitchen window at "Port Boy," in the early 1940s, but the location proved untraceable. In the mid-1940s, a family of 3 saw "a reddish-brown ape-like creature" on Hanging Rock Hill, while driving on U.S. Route 52.[17]

In August 1943, a 5-year-old boy became separated from his parents while camping in Ashland County's Mohican-Memorial State Forest. Fifty-four years later, he claimed that a "large female ape-like creature" carried him safely back to camp, while his parents were out searching for him. He drew a crude picture of the animal two months later, assisted by his kindergarten teacher.[18]

In summer 1948, a security guard at a factory in Cincinnati's Carthage suburb saw "a strange man-like figure" walking with a "shaggy dog" or "young lion." The biped reappeared on a second occasion, accompanied by two dogs: one black, one white.[19]

Witness Dean Averick saw a hairy biped at Padanaram in 1954, describing it as 6 feet tall and "very chesty," with a snub nose and "peaked eyes." The same year produced another sighting from Pandora, but no details are available and the similiarity of names may indicate an error.[20]

In 1956, a young girl playing on her grandparents' farm near Prattsville saw a Bigfoot in the yard. She kept the incident a secret until 1989, for fear of ridicule.[21]

Internet blogger Lewis DuPlatt claims that his father met a Sasquatch at some undisclosed location in Ohio, during 1956. Texas researcher Craig Woolheater challenges that claim, noting that "DuPlatt's" website is registered to a Louis Duplain, and that it displays various photos apparently lifted without credit from competing websites. DuPlatt/Duplain has not responded publicly.[22]

Christopher Murphy reports a Bigfoot sighting from Alliance, in 1957, but provides no details. In January 1958, a Noble County farmer found humanoid footprints 13 inches long and 6 inches wide, separated by a 5-foot stride, on his property near Harriettsville.[23]

A teenager checking his rabbit traps near Adario, in November 1958, met a foul-smelling biped 7 feet tall, with a face "not exactly human, but not animal either." It retreated, stepping over a 6-foot fence. Three months later, at nearby Mansfield, a 7-foot creature with gray fur and luminous eyes frightened another witness.[24]

The 1960s

The decade's first report comes from an unnamed small town near Wilmington, where a 9-foot Sasquatch barged into a house, then fled when the tenant brandished a shotgun. Peculiar noises were also reported.[25]

Sometime in 1962, a youth met a reddish-haired biped while hiking through the Audubon Wildlife Sanctuary, outside Aurora. He went public in 2002.[26]

In 1963, while parked near Cincinnati, Wallace Wright and his girlfriend saw a creature "like a huge tree walking" and alerted several other witnesses before it fled.[27]

Mansfield's gray beast with luminous eyes returned in March 1963, frightening C.W. Cox and several other witnesses.[28]

In July 1963, 3 teenage boys saw a 7-foot, reddish-brown biped described as "resembling part bear, part ape, and part human," crossing a field two miles outside Ashland. Its eyes shone pink in the beams from their flashlights.[29]

In 1964, while parked at Point Isabel, Lew Lister and his girlfriend saw a 6-foot biped with a nose and ears resembling a pig's. It passed through a barbed-wire fence "like mist," then "changed shape and vanished" after dropping to all fours. Before the disappearing act, the future Mrs. Lister "felt hypnotized" and "had a time lapse or like I was living in a different time."[30]

During the same year, residents of Cincinnati's Milford suburb claimed an "ape-like animal" had damaged property and killed cattle on farms along State Route 28.[31]

In summer 1965, a couple driving with their son through Bellefontaine saw a dark-haired biped, more than 6 feet tall and with "very long arms," walking along railroad tracks on the west side of town. They stopped to watch it pass, the husband remarking, "That thing could crush this car."[32]

In 1966, an unnamed witness reported a 7-foot "ape-man" roaming the southern portion of Wayne National Forest, which covers 834,000 acres spanning 12 counties.[33]

One night, in April 1966, while fishing at an unnamed Auglaize County river, several witnesses observed an 8-foot biped standing on a nearby bridge. It was "ape-like in stance but thinner than a gorilla [with] big red glowing eyes." It fled as they approached the bridge. A pack of hunting dogs brought to the site next day refused to track its scent.[34]

In summer 1967, two teenagers in Elyria were watching television when barking dogs drew their attention outside. They observed "something big like a large human" running and making a "terrible screaming sound," with several dogs in pursuit. The runner left large 5-toed tracks in mud.[35]

In Salem, during spring 1968, Alice Allison and son Bruce claimed several sightings of "a large, shadowy, manlike creature" surveilling their home. Once, they saw it run "so fast it did not even seem to touch the ground." Around the same time, they were haunted by a "large cat-like animal" that left 6-inch claw marks on trees and 3-inch-wide paw prints in soil.[36]

On April 22, 1968, William Schwark and a friend claimed they were assaulted by Bigfoot, with Schwark knocked down a hillside, his jacket torn and shoulder scratched. During the same month, author John Keel claimed a Sasquatch sighting in some woods behind the Cleveland Zoo.[37]

In summer 1968, 4 members of the Muncy family were frightened at their Pataskala farm by the appearance of a "tall black hairy thing," whose head towered 2 feet above a 6-foot fence.[38]

Eugene and Kathy Kline met Sasquatch on July 8, 1968, near their Elm Street home in Butler, describing the creature as 7 or 8 feet tall, with a head "3 feet in diameter." Four days later, their sister Teresa became hysterical after the red-eyed monster peered into her bedroom window. Both incidents were documented in police reports, including an observation that the beast "smelled very similar to cow shit."[39]

One night, in autumn 1968, members of the Abbott family heard a sound "like metal being hit" outside their home near Point Isabel. With neighbor Arnold Hubbard, they observed a hairy biped 10 feet tall, with shoulders 4 feet wide. Hubbard shot it with a .22-caliber rifle, whereupon it screamed and "a white mist enveloped it." When the mist cleared, it was gone.[40]

On November 9, 1968, a couple named Cataldo woke to a thump on the side of their house in Lorain. Suddenly, they saw a "huge face" at their bedroom window, with two "paws or hands" on the window sill. Mr. Cataldo scrambled for a gun, whereupon the creature fled, running upright and "weaving from side to side like an ape." Despite its means of locomotion, the Cataldos described it as "a large lion of around 600 pounds." Its palm prints on the window sill were humanoid, but "the prints were reversed and ran in a straight line," whatever that means.[41]

Christopher Murphy notes a final sighting for the decade, from Gallipolis on January 23, 1969, but offers no details.[42]

The 1970s

Our first two sightings from the Seventies — from rural Vinton County and from Pleasantville — also come from Murphy, without any more specific dates or other information.[43]

Three cases are on file from 1970. In October, a motorist nearly collided with a 7-foot biped on Fox Road, south of Huron. In November, witness "R. T." found a 100-yard trail of large humanoid footprints crossing a soybean field near Edinburgh, leading to a bloody patch of ground beside a bog. A month later, Portage County's Record-Courier described a large hairy creature running beside a car on Stroup Road, in nearby Atwater.[44]

Both of 1971's sightings occurred during summer. In June, witness "D. M." and several friends saw an "enormous" creature in the backyard of his Calcutta home. Standing beside a 15-foot tree, it appeared to be 10 feet tall. Witness "Rodney" and friends saw a large ape-like face at a window of his home near Vincent, in Wayne National Forest, then watched it flee, screaming as it stepped over a 3-strand barbed-wire fence.[45]

"IT WAS THIS BIG"—Wayne E. Lewis, a 6-foot 360-pounder, said the monster was at least a foot taller than he and weighed at least as much. Cleveland Patrolman Robert G. Yurwa, right, gets the description before starting an intensive search of the neighborhood.
Plain Dealer Photo (William G. Vorce)

Hairy 'Monster' Is Hunted in Brookside Park Area

By John P. Coyne

A "monster animal," described as more than 7-feet tall and weighing at least 360 pounds, was sought yesterday after it frightened several persons on W. 39th Street near Brookside Park.

Cleveland police and Metropolitan Park rangers searched Brookside Park and the Cleveland Zoo after several residents reported the huge black-haired monster appeared behind a fence at the south end of W. 39th Street.

The area behind the fence slopes down into Brookside Park where the zoo is located.

Wayne E. Lewis, 36, of 3861 W. 39th Street, told police he was looking for a kitten about 9:30 p.m. Saturday when he

E. Scoggins of Spartanburg, launched

looked up and saw the monster standing behind the fence.

Lewis, who is 6-feet-tall and weighs 360 pounds himself, said the monster was bigger than he.

"I RAN INTO THE HOUSE for my shotgun," Lewis said. "I didn't want to call the police because it would sound like I was some kind of fool. On the other hand. I didn't want to take any chances."

Michael I. Taub, 19, who was visiting relatives on W. 39th, said he saw the mysterious creature shake the trees behind the fence.

Taub said at first he thought it was a gorilla, but then he noticed it stood straighter than a gorilla.

Continued on Page 6, Col. 1

said.

The press reports a 1968 sighting near Cleveland's zoo.
Credit: Author's collection

Five incidents comprise the record for 1972. In mid-August, Wayne Lewis and another witness saw an apelike creature more than 6 feet tall in Brookside Park, near Cleveland's zoo. Teenager "John D." glimpsed the silhouette of a hulking biped at Mahoning County's Lake Milton marina that summer, while an Allen County farmer confronted a 6-foot, 350-pound prowler at 1:30 a.m. on October 1. November brought sightings from Dublin, where a large biped left footprints, and from Ironton, where a taxi driver told police he saw a "large white ape-like thing" dragging the carcass of a deer or dog.[46]

Six reports exist for 1973, 4 of them from August. In that busy month, a foul-smelling 8-foot monster chased 6 raccoon hunters near Oberlin; another 8-footer fled under fire from a farm at Mansfield; a 7-foot creature with glowing, red eyes visited New London, while a Massilon sighting provided no details. On October 1, the *Columbus Dispatch* reported multiple sightings of an 8-foot white-haired monster from the Jack Nicklaus golf course, then under construction near Dublin. It left 12-inch footprints, 7 inches wide. A 7-foot stinker reappeared at Massilon, in October, but eluded police.[47]

Five cases emerged from 1974, starting with vague reports of a Bigfoot "supposedly seen" at an East Canton strip mine, and another spotted at Ashtabula City sometime "between 1974 and 1979." That spring, 2 youths hunting turtles on the Little Portage River, near Port Clinton, saw a hairy biped wading through a marsh. In September, 14-inch humanoid footprints were photographed in a field near Westerville. In October, an Auglaize County raccoon hunter heard strange screams near St. Marys, then was knocked down by a biped carrying a deer over its shoulder. The creature dropped its kill, which had part of one leg "twisted almost completely off."[48]

The year 1975 offers two cases, one an undated report of "unusual dome structures" found in Hamilton County. Such artifacts, possibly nests, prompt some researchers to dub Ohio's Bigfoot the "Grassman." On July 10, 1975, 3 pre-teen children saw a hairy biped watching them over the tops of 6-foot corn stalks on a Preble County farm.[49]

Ten reports made 1976 a busier year. The first (undated) case involves a sighting with footprints near Eaton. Two policemen had separate sightings of Bigfoot at Woodlawn, in February. On April 4, several fishermen saw a "large baboon" near the Little Miami River, at Milford (a Cincinnati suburb), while others heard strange cries in the woods. That summer, 2 girls found 15-inch footprints beside Aurora Lake. In July, several youths wading in the Olentangy River south of Delaware saw a huge biped covered in reddish-brown hair on the river bank. August brought sightings of a creature 8 to 9 feet tall, with 3-foot-wide shoulders, from a farm near Canton, and another—smaller than a man, with a "slightly pointed

head"—from Carroll County's Atwood
Lake campground. In September, a
child from Wadsworth met Bigfoot
crouching in the woods. November's
sighting came from Monroe Township,
where a rabbit hunter glimpsed a
massive creature "running on 2 feet full
steam ahead."[50]

Thirteen cases were logged in 1977.
The first, undated, was a motorist's
sighting of a 9-foot biped standing in a
ditch beside Coy Road, two miles south
of Ney. February brought two reports:
Jackie Smith found 20-inch footprints in
snow, near Hamilton, while 2 women
driving through Noble County saw an
8-foot creature running along County
Road 19. On March 8, 2 teenagers fired
shots at an 8-foot hairy biped in Nelson.
Neighbor Barbara Pistilli told police
the creature had been seen before.
The same month brought 2 sightings
from Alliance, where a Sasquatch with
"bright yellow eyes" frightened drivers,
leaving footprints behind. On May 18,
teenagers "D. B." and "T. L." saw a
9-foot, 500-pound creature near Preble
County's Roberts Covered Bridge.
A local farmer subsequently found
2 footprints on his property, while
authors Colin and Janet Bord report
"more Bigfoot sightings" from Eaton on
May 21. Several children saw a female
Sasquatch with prominent breasts near
Sparta, that summer, and our Ottawa
County witness, from 1974, heard
strange cries "like a scream, howl, and
yodel all rolled into one" around the
same time. Several Boy Scouts glimpsed
a Bigfoot with "piercing green eyes" at
Camp Oyo, in late autumn. December
brought another sighting from Eaton,
with footprints and "unusual odors."[51]

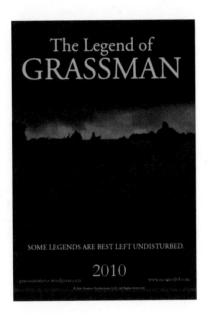

Poster for a film based on Ohio
"Grassman" sightings.
Credit: Author's collection

The year 1978 produced at least 35 Bigfoot reports, including major flaps in Richland and Stark Counties. Undated reports include 3 separate sightings of a "muscular and massive" creature by "Angela X" and her sons near Utopia. In January, 3 Morrow County hunters saw a "freak of nature bear" walking on two legs, stepping over a 5-foot fence. A month later, 2 brothers glimpsed a creature more than 6 feet tall at Newbury. The action heated up in June, as Bigfoot spooked 4 young hikers near Somerset, surprised a mini-bike rider at Fulton, made a young berry-picker faint in Clermont County, and harassed a family in rural Jackson County.[52]

A "large baboon" was seen at Milford in 1976.
Credit: U.S. Fish & Wildlife Service

Monster mania struck Richland County in June, when a motorist blamed his car crash on a Sasquatch bolting across State Route 95. That same month, Butler Police Chief Phil Stortz acknowledged "half a dozen" sightings from his town. Members of the Kline family logged 3 sightings of a beast they dubbed "Bighead" on July 8, 10, and 12, while multiple unrelated witnesses met Bigfoot in Butler, on July 9, and near Bellville on the 10th.[53]

Before tempers had time to cool in Richland, Sasquatch moved east, to Stark County. In July, two brothers at Navarre reported foul odors and "low-pitched growls that became high-pitched screams." Herbert Cayton's family and various neighbors logged their first Sasquatch sighting on August 20, 2 miles west of Minerva. The creature returned with 2 "cougar-type" cats on the 21st, then came again without its pets on the 22nd and 23rd. Brothers John and Jerry Nutter tried to photograph the beast, without success, on August 26, but they directed police to several large footprints. Mary Ackerman reported 2 hairy bipeds lurking around a local strip mine on September 8. The next day, Henry Colt saw Bigfoot 5 miles east of his Minerva home. A few nights later, the Caytons endured one last nocturnal visit.[54]

Summer 1978 produced one more sighting, from Layman, where two young siblings saw a "stooped over" biped trudging through woods near their home. A fisherman suspected Bigfoot after hearing strange vocalizations along Twin Creek in September, but blamed an unnamed neighbor for hoaxing footprints earlier. The same month, in Tallmadge, a child playing hide-and-seek with friends found Sasquatch instead. Two witnesses driving on Poe Road, near Medina, saw a 6-foot creature at roadside, in autumn. Finally, in November, a child reported a rank-smelling biped, 7 feet tall, prowling his family's land near Marietta.[55]

Ten more reports complete the decade's tally. Undated cases from 1979 include a sighting by Herbert Burke Jr. at a trailer park in Paris Township, and a London sighting logged by a minister and 5 of his parishioners. Beverly Fletcher found 3 large footprints in snow, at Bloomingdale in January, while a sighting from Cuyahoga Falls on January 9 is sadly devoid of details. A farming family at Haydenville was frightened by a brush with Sasquatch in May. Ronald Chamberlin saw a "husky, hairy creature, larger than a dog," in July, crossing State Route 296 near Urbana. Scott Simpson saw a 6-foot biped near his home in North Lewisburg on October 7, with 10-inch "pigeon-toed" tracks left behind. A witness named Sheets saw Sasquatch near his Wapakoneta home in winter 1979, accompanied by 18-inch footprints with a 7.5-foot stride. Two cases dated only from the "late 1970s" involve discovery of humanoid tracks at Minerva and near Mingo Junction.[56]

The 1980s

This decade's Bigfoot tales begin with 5 undated reports. Five hikers claimed a meeting with 2 bipeds more than 8 feet tall, outside Urbana, while 2 separate sightings were filed from London. Informant "Keith Z." reports "several sightings" around Elyria, early in the Eighties, and mentions articles from the local *Chronicle Telegram*, but provides no useful specifics. A Marietta witness from 1978 also recalls discovery of footprints 17 to 20 inches long, sometime before 1983.[57]

Four incidents from 1980 also lack specific dates. Christopher Murphy logs sightings at the Simpson farm, outside North Lewisburg; another at Marysville; and a report of 19-inch footprints near London. A camper in Mohican State Park, near Chardon, also saw "a young Bigfoot," around 5 feet, 7 inches tall, covered in grayish-brown hair.[58]

Another 38 incidents with more specific dates make 1980 one of Ohio's busiest years for biped encounters. In March, 18-inch tracks appeared in the snow around Woodstock. A family in Rome sighted a "gorilla-like" creature in June, then found 4 of their ducks decapitated. West Mansfield produced 2 June sightings of a 7-foot biped, while a stinking 6-foot creature left 16-inch tracks at nearby Russell's Point. Columbiana County also logged 2 sightings in June, from a residence on Beaver Creek and another on a farm between Calcutta and East Liverpool.[59]

On June 17, while plowing a field in Union County, farmer Patrick Poling saw a 7-foot creature described as "a big hairy ape that walked like a man." The next day, with neighbors, he made plaster casts of tracks 17 inches long and 7 inches wide. On June 22, residents of rural Logan County fled from a "hulking shape" in the woods, and Russell's Point policeman Ray Quay met a 7-foot prowler in his barnyard, reporting that it "smelled like Limburger cheese on a hot muffler."[60]

Two days later, Donna Riegler found a creature lying on the road near Marysville. Rising as she approached, it "stumbled away with a robot-like walk." Logan County farmer Larry Hamey met Bigfoot while tilling his fields, on June 26.[61]

July 1980 brought reports from Lisbon, where an "unusual creature" left 15-inch tracks; North Lewisburg, on the Simpson farm; from a Stark County hiker, who met a shrieking "hairy thing" at a strip mine near Navarre; from 3 fishermen near Clarksburg, who saw an 8-foot beast that smelled "like a mixture of something that had been decaying in the sun covered in rotten eggs"; from Nelsonville's Hocking Technical College, where 3 students met a 7-foot monster that smelled like "wet dogs"; and from Plain City, where Charles Lovejoy, Ron Winn, and others encountered a 7-foot beast on July 15.[62]

August was another hectic month, with 7 reports. A sighting in Wayne National Forest produced footprints, 2 friends saw a 6-foot creature in Geauga County's Russell Township, and 2 siblings saw something of similar size running along County Road 22 in Lawrence County. Larry Cottrill claimed 2 Vinton County sightings, on August 11 and 24. Three creatures appeared on the second occasion, leaving 17.5-inch tracks, Cottrill asserting that he wounded Bigfoot with rifle fire. Between those incidents, a "young Bigfoot" startled campers in Ashland County, on August 12, and a couple from Cambridge saw "a creature with Bigfoot characteristics" in Salt Fork State Park, on the 18th. A final summer case vaguely refers to "giant red-eyed ape-like creatures" seen around West Jefferson.[63]

Sasquatch took September off, then returned for a busy October. Witness "Ron" claimed 3 separate sightings that month, while hunting around Ash Cave in Hocking Hills State Park. A witness saw Bigfoot near Lima, where investigators later found feces containing berry seeds, hair, and wood bark, analyzed by a forensic lab as coming from "a human-type digestive tract." Rodney Peoples—a neighbor of Larry Cottrill in Vinton County—reported sightings of a 9-foot creature on October 5 and 10; investigators found footprints and "possible Bigfoot blood" at the second location.[64]

Ash Cave, scene of a 1980 Bigfoot sighting.
Credit: U.S. Geological Survey

The year ends with 3 reports from autumn and "late 1980." A teenager heard eerie cries and saw "a huge hairy thing on 2 feet" at his home, on State Route 22 between Bloomingdale and Wintersville, and a boy in Scioto County had a similar experience, in the southwestern part of the Shawnee State Forest. Finally, a vague sighting report from Marysville offers no details.[65]

Four undated cases begin our list for 1981. Witnesses "Jim" and "Kathy" met an 8-foot biped while horseback riding in Colerain Township; a deputy sheriff claimed 2 sightings at Bellefontaine; and Lima's Mammal Research Team found 15-inch tracks near a Van Wert County farm where 40-odd piglets were killed over a 6-month period.[66]

On January 31, 1981, 3 hikers found a 16-inch footprint, 8 inches wide, on a sandbar near Peebles. March brought another sighting from North Lewisburg. Rock Creek produced 2 sightings in June; at the second, a witness reported wounding Bigfoot with a shotgun. Two residents of Rome chased Sasquatch with guns on June 29, then retreated on seeing "3 pairs of large eyes." Shining eyes and darting UFOs sparked more gunfire in Rome on July 1, followed by sightings of 2 black bipeds on July 3, a single creature that left "strange prints" on July 6, and another one-sided shootout with a 12-foot prowler on July 7. Four London residents, investigating strange lights in the sky, suffered damage to their car from a hulking creature, while a woman saw Bigfoot at Paine Falls Metro Park, and another glimpsed a biped near her home in Columbia Station. On July 16, another sighting occurred at West Jefferson.[67]

Darke County produced a multiple-witness sighting of Bigfoot in August, while Columbiana residents logged an encounter that month, and another in September 1981. On October 9, 3 young witnesses met a "huge black form" at Rock Creek, where searchers later found "peculiar footprints." November brought 2 sightings: of an 8-foot biped in Hanover Township, and another beast that left footprints in Champaign County.[68]

The year 1982's reports begin with 20-inch tracks near Marietta, found by a witness who saw Bigfoot in 1978. On March 4, in Medina County, 3 young hunters met "a stocky monkey" in the woods. June brought sightings of "a huge silhouette" at Crooked Tree, and a crouching "monkey-type animal" near Calcutta, in Beaver Creek State Park. In July, Bigfoot was seen in the Shawnee State Forest, near Portsmouth, and by witness "D. M." in Columbiana. In November, 3 witnesses watched a 7-foot biped cross a highway near Sidney. The following month, one of the same witnesses saw a foul-smelling creature in her yard.[69]

Five reports exist for 1983. In May, multiple witnesses saw Bigfoot and found its tracks on a farm southwest of Mechanicsburg. That summer, witness "D. T." met a large biped near Mogadore Reservoir. October produced reports of "a loud scream and an awful smell" from Byhalia, and a discovery of 2 "huge" footprints separated by a 6-foot stride, near Mechanicsburg. Finally, that autumn, a witness who reported wild vocalizations in spring 1974, heard something "very similar" near Clyde.[70]

Seven incidents comprise our record for 1984. Undated reports include a sighting with footprints from Cincinnati Municipal Lunken Airport, a 7-foot creature seen at Charles Mill Lake, and a window-peeping incident northwest of Minerva. On January 15, outside Claylick, 2 girls saw a creature "baboon like in appearance, but much larger in size." On July 2, a woman and her 3 children saw a grinning Sasquatch near Sharonville. An albino biped appeared near Churchtown on July 4. Two boys saw Bigfoot at Mineral Ridge, on November 12.[71]

Seven reports are known from 1985. Four boys from London claimed 3 separate, undated sightings. A Kent State University student heard apelike vocalizations near campus on April 16. Three hunters met an 8-foot creature with a "horrid odor" in June, near Twin Valley. Betty Powell claims she fed 3 hairy bipeds at her West Jefferson home, in September. On September 15, researcher Don Keating logged a personal sighting 4 miles south of Newcomerstown.[72]

Reports for 1986 start with a vague, undated sighting at Xenia. A fisherman sighted a "huge, hairy monster" in June or July, at Mount Orab. A "very black" biped frightened residents of Georgetown in July. Later that summer, a man in Kent heard an "incredibly loud howling sound" that "suggested an animal in pain." In October, 3 teens saw Bigfoot crouched beside Timlin Road, in Portsmouth. Autumn brought a hunter's report of dogs chasing a 9-foot brown biped, east of Hamden.[73]

Our 5 reports from 1987 start in March, with a nocturnal sighting on Lima's Lost Creek Golf Course. In May, a fisherman saw "a huge white thing" swimming in Antrim Lake, then jogging off into the woods. Reverend Lee Birt saw Sasquatch near Woodstock in August, collecting strands of brown hair that remained unidentified after testing at Ohio State University. On August 7, horseback riders saw a "dark shape," noting its "nasty smell and a loud moaning scream" between Bergholz and Monroeville. October witnessed a teenage hunter's meeting with a large grunting biped near Oberlin.[74]

Ten reports kept investigators busy in 1988. Undated cases include a sighting from Akron, and a report of 2 creatures seen by a father and son "in winter," at Smithfield's Friendship Park. On January 1, Bigfoot was spotted in Coshocton. Witness "Steve" found 11.5-inch tracks outside Warsaw on May 15, preserving them with plaster casts. In June, 2 young couples fled from a snarling black biped outside Sandyville. Two months later, a policeman hunting near Batesville heard vocalizations "identical" to purported recordings of Sasquatch. Two trappers heard similar sounds around Bellville and Butler, from mid-August to early September. In the latter month, 2 boys reported Bigfoot lobbing stones at them, near Urichsville, and a Germantown resident saw one lurking near his home on the 15th. During winter, ice fishermen at Friendship Lake watched 2 albino bipeds carrying some object "the size of a pickup truck's bed."[75]

Five reports from 1989 include 3 without dates: sightings at Xenia and Minerva, plus a "high-pitched kind of roar" disrupting a family picnic at Prattsville. In August, 3 hikers saw a white Sasquatch at Highbanks Metro Park, in Lewis Center. A screaming biped visited a farm near South Vienna on Thanksgiving Day (November 23). Finally, Barbersville resident Barbara Bilinovich says 3 "humongous" bipeds chased her through the woods one night, in the "late 1980s."[76]

The 1990s

The new decade started slowly, with 2 reports from 1990. During summer, 3 boys saw a large biped cross their yard, 4 miles from Barlow. In October, teenage campers saw a red-eyed, 7-foot Sasquatch in the Shawnee State Forest.[77]

Seven cases from 1991 begin with 3 undated incidents: a Prattsville farmer fled his field at the appearance of a creature with a "pungent, musty smell, strong and nauseating"; a Logan County hunter watched an 8-foot biped pass below his tree stand; while Craig Young and his wife met a beast with a "flat face like a monkey, all wrinkled looking," near Liverpool. On February 24, 4 campers saw Sasquatch and found its 16-inch tracks near Ironton. In July, a mother and son saw an 8-foot creature cross Austin Road in Geneva. A screaming creature chased 2 Ashland County teenagers in September, leaving one with the impression that it "had to have been at least 16 feet tall!" On November 25, a "slim muscular" biped frightened a hunter at Plainfield.[78]

Reports are sparse for 1992. Don Keating reports finding footprints in several sizes near Moscow, in June, and claims he accidentally videotaped a white biped at the same location on August 2 (though he did not view the tape until December 1993). In September a motorist glimpsed a 7-foot creature on River Styx Road, near Medina. Two months later, hunter "Mike" found 3 deer carcasses in rural Stark County, with 14-inch footprints nearby. A December Bigfoot sighting, from Guernsey County, also involved a mutilated deer.[79]

Cases from 1993 begin with an undated sighting of something "dark and tall" crossing a Guernsey County road. One witness to that incident also claimed he was "attacked by a Bigfoot 4 or 5 years prior," escaping with torn clothing and "a big hand print across his

face and back." In summer 1993, a farmer reported finding a collection of severed deer legs, neatly arranged in a cave near Wills Creek, south of Coshocton. While loitering there, he saw Sasquatch approaching and hastily fled. In June, a father and son in Fostoria heard screams "identical" to purported Bigfoot recordings. Five witnesses reported a silver-gray creature peering through their windows near Donnelsville, in late August or early September. Matt Moneymaker reports "several" sightings around Berlin Lake, in Ohio, but offers no details. In autumn, a Brown County hunter glimpsed Bigfoot from his tree stand.[80]

Four cases comprise our file for 1994. In February, Scott McCaslin saw Bigfoot at Woodsfield, locating 3-toed tracks with 8-foot strides. On February 12, a fisherman sighted a hairy biped at Jay Lake, in West Branch State Park. In summer, "Rick J." and his sister met 2 "huge" creatures while biking around strip mines near Atwater. In September, hunter Ryan Lehman saw a Sasquatch running through woods outside Nelsonville.[81]

Shawnee State Forest has produced multiple Bigfoot sightings
Credit: U.S. Geological Survey

Six of our 18 reports from 1995 are undated. They include a teenager's sighting of a red-eyed creature near McClure, an encounter with a white biped at Flushing, a Sasquatch appearance near Akron; a discovery of 17-inch footprints in Wayne State Forest, a claim that Bigfoot chased 2 hunters near Trenton, and a Brown County couple's encounter with Sasquatch along the Ohio River.[82]

In February 1995, a driver and her passenger saw Bigfoot drinking from a roadside pond near North Industry. On March 11, a resident of Sagamore Hills saw a 7-foot creature moving "fast, in a weird way." April brought a sighting from Newcomerstown and a report of footprints near Flushing. In May, an Adams County hunter saw Sasquatch and found its 10-inch handprint in mud. During summer, campers near Prattsville reported strange sounds in the night. Three hikers met Bigfoot in Cuyahoga Valley National Park on July 4. Two days later, more tracks appeared around Flushing. In September, a Sedamsville fisherman reported a sighting near the Ohio River. A motorist saw Sasquatch 4 miles south of Hiram, in October. Ron Brunner saw a hairy biped on his farm at Alliance, in December. Around the same time, tracks were found and photographed near Madisonville.[83]

We have 9 reports on file from 1996. In March, a Brown County farmer's wife logged the first of several sightings on her property. On March 17, a woman in Newcomerstown saw 2 bipeds — an 8-footer and a smaller "juvenile." While investigating that report, Don Keating heard the tale of a driver who allegedly found a Sasquatch dead on the road, at some undisclosed Ohio site. Police were followed to the scene by 3 uniformed soldiers in a van, who removed the carcass to parts unknown. Researchers found 10-inch, 3-toed tracks near Eaton on April 6. July brought a hunter's sighting from rural Adams County. Two witnesses reported Sasquatch on a road near Eaton, on August 16, and investigators briefly glimpsed it 12 days later. Matt Christian heard "odd whistling sounds" and "a loud, distant-sounding groan" outside Ontario, that summer. In October, a hunter caught Bigfoot watching him, near Boden, and found footprints larger than his size-13 EEE boots.[84]

Sixteen reports from 1997 begin with 4 undated incidents. A family living near Newcomerstown claimed 3 encounters with a reddish-brown biped that uttered "gorilla-like screams," while more strange howls accompanied discovery of footprints outside Cable. A teacher saw Bigfoot cross the road near Hubbard, in January, and photographed its 15-inch footprint in snow. Jackie Smith found more tracks around Butler, the following month. April brought reports of ape-like vocalizations from Kent and Utopia.[85]

One Saturday in mid-June 1997, a motorist saw Bigfoot cross Williams Road in Columbus. Local television aired another sighting one week later. On July 3, 10 canoers glimpsed a 7-foot biped beside the Mohican River, near Loudonville. In autumn, a photographer heard simian screams at Beaver Creek State Park, and a hunter saw a creature "bigger than a person" outside Wintersville. Two hunters watched Sasquatch cross a field near Peebles with "astonishing speed," in November. The same month, a woman caught Bigfoot standing beside a dumpster in Youngstown, where it left tracks in light snow. On December 12, Sasquatch peered through the window of a home at Lynx, leaving 16-inch tracks in the yard.[86]

Another 14 reports for 1998 start with a sighting by 4 young men, near Westminster. In March, 2 hikers found freshly-killed beavers in the Woodbury Wildlife Area, with 16-inch, 3-toed footprints nearby. May produced 3 incidents: campers found tracks after a night of harassment in Wayne National Forest; a fisherman saw a short biped walking beside the Auglaize River, near Defiance, on the 24th; and witness "R. D." glimpsed a 7-footer while camped 5 miles from Tappan Lake, on the 30th.[87]

In July 1998, a driver watched Bigfoot drag a dead animal across State Route 45, below North Jackson. On July 11th Sasquatch surprised a visitor to an old cemetery near Logan. Two hikers photographed, foot, hand, and knuckle prints in mud near Birds Run, on August 15th. September brought a sighting from Wayne National Forest on Labor Day weekend, another from Richfield, and a discovery of 15-inch tracks between Bellville and Butler. Three campers saw a 7-foot monster near Enon, in October, while a hunter saw a "fat" white biped at Birds Run, on October 15th. The year ends with a hunter's report of "wood-knocking" sounds near Nelsonville, on November 19th.[88]

The decade closes with 22 reports from 1999. On February 20, witness "Mrs. J." saw Bigfoot cross a rural road in Muskingum County. Two boys fled from "a monster-looking thing" in Jefferson Township, on April 26. In May, a motorist saw Sasquatch standing beside U.S. Route 6 in Ashtabula County. On May 25, the *Portsmouth Daily Times* published Dallas Gilbert's claim of 9 recent sightings in Scioto County. A fisherman caught a 7-foot creature watching him in Shelby County, on June 15. In July, the husband of a Lake Tappan witness from 1998 woke to foul odors around their camp, at the same location. Four witnesses saw a 7-foot biped with "a Darth Vader head" and found its footprints, while camped on July 24 at an undisclosed site in northeastern Ohio. Summer ended with August reports of a New London sighting with footprints and vocalizations, a 400-yard trail of footprints in West Branch State Park, and screams that left 3 campers sleepless near Senecaville.[89]

Four more reports complete the year and decade. In October, the same hunter who reported wood-knocking around Nelsonville, heard screams and guttural moans near the same location. Sometime in autumn, a Warsaw resident saw "a brown bear" climb a hillside "walking upright on 2 legs." Witness "J. S." found twenty 18-inch footprints near Lima, on November 1. Witness "K. B." and a friend met Bigfoot on Green Ridge Road, in Latham, on December 22.[90]

The 21st Century

2000-2012

The new century started strong, with 18 reports for 2000. The first, undated, describes Bigfoot kneeling to drink from Meander Reservoir, in Austintown. Wild nocturnal screams roused Leavittsburg residents on February 13 and 14, while a large black creature left footprints in snow at Mosquito Lake Park. May's reports include a fisherman's sighting of 2 bipeds near Waverly, a farmer's discovery of large tracks near Warsaw on May 7, and a teen's claim that a "tall hairy creature" chased his motorcycle near Hamden, late in the month.[91]

Summer's incidents begin with a sighting on June 29, by 3 witnesses who saw Sasquatch strolling through the Rock Mill Dam Wildlife Area. On August 9 a hiker found a 20-inch footprint in Bazetta Township. Four days later, a trucker watched a reddish-colored biped cross a road in Wayne National Forest. Dana Chesser found 3-toed footprints outside Tipp City, on September 1, and heard "loud chirping-whistles" nearby, while her young son claimed a sighting of a hairy giant.[92]

October 2000 produced 4 reports: campers saw a large gray biped at Tappan Lake; a motorist glimpsed a brown Bigfoot near Wadsworth; a repeat witness from Clark County logged his third sighting since 1993, near Enon; and 2 hunters met a screaming hairy creature in the Resthaven Wildlife Area, on the 29th. Bigfoot frightened another hunter near Donnelsville, on November 24. On December 28, 2 witnesses saw a pair of gray 8-foot bipeds on Timberwoods Road, near Geneva.[93]

Fifteen cases comprise the record for 2001. A man who reported tracks and screams from Cable in 1997 claimed a similar incident this year, in the same vicinity. Witness "D. O." and a friend saw Bigfoot running through woods near East Canton, on February 24. A Bainbridge resident claimed the first of 3 personal sightings in March, while recording a neighbor's report of 6 bipeds roaming together. He refrained from further description, saying, "There is too much to tell. I could write a book."

In April, 2 hikers near Coshocton blamed Bigfoot for leaving muskrat carcasses "in a possible display arrangement."[94]

Five summer reports begin in June, at Steubenville, where a newlywed couple heard "strange and diverse" animal cries outside their home. That same month, 2 witnesses saw a smelly biped "7 feet or taller" near Governor Bebb Preserve. James Good was fishing at Lake Vesuvius, in July, when he saw an 8-foot creature that smelled "like a wet dog." Later that month, a witness watched Bigfoot cross State Route 170 near Fredericktown. Sasquatch allegedly attacked 2 hikers at Mineral Ridge, on August 19, ripping the man's shirt and grabbing his daughter's leg before they escaped.[95]

A reddish-brown creature, 7 feet tall, appeared on a farm near Lodi, in September 2001. Two boys saw an 8-foot biped near Meander Creek Reservoir, on October 10, and the same month brought a second sighting from a Hanover Township witness who first glimpsed Bigfoot in 1981. November caps the year with 2 reports—of a "screaming ape-like creature" seen near Rogers, and another seen by motorist Russ Gower in Cascade Valley Park, "on or near Thanksgiving" (November 22).[96]

Twenty-one reports are on record for 2002. The first, undated, describes a large black biped howling and reeking near Cable. January brought 2 reports of footprints: a 200-yard trail found by Tom Caleodis in Linton Township, on the 11th, and a 400-yard series discovered at an undisclosed location in eastern Ohio. On February 19, a motorist and her son saw a large "white-yellowish" creature crossing a road on all fours, near Columbiana. Loren Greer and Dana Smith saw Bigfoot outside their Bentonville home on February 23, and found its 17-inch footprints the next morning. Cheryl Barger heard screams "identical" to supposed Bigfoot calls outside her Clermont County home on March 13; 2 days later, her brother-in-law saw a bipedal creature nearby.[97]

One of Steubenville's witnesses from 2001 reported banging sounds, a smell like rotting garbage, and discovery of footprints near her home in May 2002. Between May 16 and 26, strange cries were heard repeatedly— and a birdfeeder was vandalized—at a home on Haga Ridge Road, near Wayne National Forest. On June 1, a driver on Interstate 675 saw a "slim" 8-foot creature in a cornfield, near Beavercreek. Okeana residents saw Bigfoot and found its tracks on July 14. Nocturnal howling was reported from Newcomerstown the following day. On July 18, a Hardin County youth saw a "huge hairy ape-looking thing" beneath a bridge spanning the Scioto River. August's reports include a sighting by 2 motorists near Mount Gilead, and a second sighting from a 1980 witness, reported from Geauga County on August 4.[98]

In September, 3 hunters saw a "large hairy ape" on a farm near Hiram, and campers outside Waverly were pelted with stones by a prowler who smelled like "wet dog." Wood-knocking sounds troubled 2 hikers near Dundee, on October 12, while 4 hunters heard "a growl that turned into a scream" near Malaga, 3 days later. A Mantua family reported frequent nocturnal howls in November, and Don Keating logged "a large number of Bigfoot sightings" the same month, including one report of a biped whose eyes were set "a sledge hammer head apart." On December 1, near Bainbridge, a hunter met a shaggy 7-foot creature emitting "a terrible smell like a rotting carcass or garbage."[99]

Reports continued apace in 2003, for 14 in all. The first, undated, was a Bigfoot sighting logged by a Sagamore Hills policeman. In February, 2 motorists reported Sasquatch walking along State Route 56, near London. A Savannah resident found large tracks near his home in March, reported "scary sounds" accompanied by "the worst B. O. smell I have ever smelled" on April 7, and found another huge footprint the following weekend. May's sightings included a "large hunched-over creature" seen near Lodi; a "hairy humanlike face" glimpsed in headlights outside Moxahala, on the 11th; and an apelike figure sprawled on Interstate 77 near Cambridge, 4 days later.[100]

On June 18, 2003, a couple hiking in Shawnee State Park found 15-inch footprints. A couple living near Zanesville watched "a tall black creature walking on 2 legs" across their property, on July 26. Two Butler County fishermen, allegedly pursued by Bigfoot back in 1995, heard its warbling cries again on August 22. Two equestriennes met an 8-foot biped that summer, in Beaver Creek State Park. On September 3, 4 teens watched a snorting creature 10 to 12 feet tall cross a cornfield near Tipp City. A witness from Ravenna claimed a sighting on October 10, described as one of "many different occasions with the creature I have dubbed 'Fang.'"[101]

Thirteen reports were filed in 2004. The first, from March, involves a Bigfoot sighting by 3 motorists on State Route 117, near Westminster. Sounds "like a woman screaming" accompanied an April 3 sighting off Clear Creek Road, near the former town of Revenge. Twelve-inch footprints appeared in Salt Fork State Park on April 15, followed by eerie howling 2 days later. Sasquatch peered through windows of a home near McArthur, on June 20, then pounded the walls hard enough to dislodge an interior shelf. Weird cries "loud as hell" frightened fishermen at Tappan Lake, in July, and roused weekenders from their cabins near Dennison on the 17th. August finished the year with a rash of sightings: of a "monkey man" in Auburn Township; by a hiker near East Farmington on the 7th; by a motorist at Huber Heights on the 15th; of 2 hairy bipeds outside Pleasant City, on the 17th; and by 2 picnickers in Salt Fork State Park, the following day. Three Portage County hunters reported a last summer sighting, of "a large hairy ape" seen near Hiram, in September.[102]

Eleven reports for 2005 begin with an undated sighting at White Oak Creek, near Sardinia. An 8-foot prowler spooked 2 campers outside Cardington, on January 13. In February, 2 motorists saw Bigfoot north of Germantown, and another spotted one near Chardon, on the 24th. Two fishermen found footprints and heard "a horrible scream" near Windham, in March. On May 30, "deep howling sounds" preceded a sighting at Malvern's Pride Valley Mobile Home Park. A driver saw Bigfoot near Sagamore Hills on July 12. Sasquatch "stalked" a fisherman at Salt Fork Lake on August 12, and startled a motorist near Chesterland on the 14th. A tourist passing through Jefferson County noted "an awesome smell" on September 1, but claimed no sighting. Two weeks later, another driver saw Sasquatch on Interstate 271, near the Boston Mills Ski Resort.[103]

Reports dwindled to 6 in 2006. A couple living near North Jackson saw a "very tall, wide-shouldered, very built" creature in April. In May, Dallas Gilbert snapped 4 blurry photos of a pale, upright figure at some undisclosed Buckeye location. A hiker glimpsed a creature 8 to 10 feet tall on July 28, in Salt Fork State Park. Bigfoot visited an Auburn Township

Tappan Lake, another site of reported Bigfoot encounters.
Credit: U.S. Geological Survey

home on August 4, and again the next day. On November 10, a brown 7-foot creature moaned and growled at a hiker in Fairfield County.[104]

Our sole report for 2007 dates from September 22. A Saybrook resident returning with her son from a shopping excursion heard "woot-woot" sounds and smelled "an awful dead animal smell like rotted skunk" before sighting a bipedal creature 6 to 7 feet tall, with "considerably long arms." Fearing ridicule, she did not report the incident until March 2011.[105]

Seven cases emerge from 2008. A former marine and his son allegedly dropped Bigfoot with pistol shots in February, in the Egypt Valley Wildlife Area, but it apparently revived and fled before they returned with police. A Geauga County fisherman glimpsed Sasquatch beside the Cuyahoga River, on May 1. Mogadore Reservoir produced a Bigfoot sighting on June 8, and claims that some growling beast stoned campers on the 10th. An 8-footer resembling "an oversized man with hair" surfaced in a New Philadelphia cornfield on June 20, and a "very tall" biped was seen in Columbiana County on July 3. A fisherman reported wood-knocking, howling, and "a strange foul smell" from Waynesville, on August 18.[106]

Thirteen cases kept investigators busy in 2009. A family at Sardinia led off with 3 undated incidents involving "strange whoops," banging on their walls, and a "God-awful wail scream that sent chills down my spine." On May 10, cries "characteristic" of Bigfoot frightened campers near Mechanicstown. June's incidents include a sighting of 2 hulking silhouettes in a farmer's field near Georgetown, and a report from fishermen who dodged a howling creature's shower of stones in East Fork Lake State Park. Ashland County hikers heard loud moans on July 25, then were pelted with rocks a week later, near the same location. A Beloit resident caught Bigfoot rattling the door to his shed in August, while September 9 produced 2 reports from Wilmington, involving vocalizations, foul odors, and broken tree limbs. On Halloween, hikers found a large footprint near Marietta, returning to cast it in plaster the following day. A video clip posted to YouTube on November 16, allegedly from Geneva, included several unconvincing snapshots and a lackluster interview with a supposed witness, accompanied by the "reporter's" comment, "This guy's probably crazy."[107]

TriState Bigfoot, founded in 2009, weighs in at this point with 3 files dated "throughout 2010 and 2011, peak activity throughout the summer months." Compounding the confusion, all describe anonymous reports from the vicinity of Mount Orab. According to the files, "Homeowners report everything from visual encounters to strange howls coming from the forest. Homeowners report seeing several (estimated 3) Sasquatch creatures in a potential 'family unit.' Homeowners report creatures peering in their window at night when the television is on and 'knocking' loudly on the brick exterior of the home. Homeowners report seeing large footprints in the mud, creek bed, and even in the snow during the winter time." Furthermore, "At one point, an investigator saw something we have been unable to identify as a human being or otherwise thus far."[108]

More concrete incidents for 2010 begin in January, with the Brown County Bigfoot Project's report of "several sighting reports including areas like Ripley, Aberdeen, and Eagle Creek." On July 6, "something very large" invaded a camp in Shawnee State Forest and lobbed a stick at one of the campers. A yellow-eyed creature prowled around a Williamsburg farm in September, tapping on windows. On October 9, a nature photographer "accidentally" snapped 2 (still unpublished) photos of an unknown biped at Ramona Lake, in Sugar Grove's Clear Creek Nature Preserve. A motorist saw Sasquatch west of Alliance, on October 22, while a fisherman glimpsed something "extremely large and jet black colored" climbing a hillside near Morrow 8 days later. On November 18 a witness in Bath heard cries "resembling" purported recordings of Bigfoot. "Loud groaning wailing calls" unnerved a group of men tracking their lost dogs near Atwater, on December 15.[109]

Ten reports from 2011 begin with a motorist's sighting of Bigfoot near Cheshire, on February 22. March brought a sighting of "2 big ones and a little one" from Mount Orab. Near Geneva, on July 15, a man collecting firewood saw "a big hairy upright creature" cross a nearby road in 4 steps. Campers engaged in a tree-knocking "conversation" with some unknown prowler near Williamsburg, in August, and Sasquatch frightened a woman at Hocking Hills State Park on August 29. Also in August, investigator Sharon Lee interviewed a "colorful" Londonderry resident who claimed repeated contacts with Sasquatch. A Fayetteville woman dodged a nocturnal shower of stones in September, while a Williamsburg witness heard "strange howls" and smelled an odor "similar to decaying grass" in September. TriState Bigfoot members heard "a strange yell/scream" near Williamsburg on October 22. The year closed with discovery of a 17-inch footprint at Williamsburg, in December, with "a huge chunk of deer hair sitting on top of a grass mound" nearby.[110]

The first sightings of 2012 were reported in January, from Mount Orab. One witness described loud vocalizations, accompanied by "sounds like a large creature moving in the brush," while another glimpsed Bigfoot crossing railroad tracks on the outskirts of town.[111] On March 24, in Mahoning County, while crossing the I-80 bridge over Meander Reservoir, a motorist glimpsed "a huge figure standing flush with the treeline" below. [BFRO #40715] In April, a video clip uploaded to YouTube appeared to show "a large, hairy creature scuffling through some trees…somewhere in northeastern Ohio," clutching a stick in one hand. [*Christian Post* (Washington, D.C.) April 27, 2012.] The original poster — believed to be researcher Ryan LeDoux — subsequently claimed that the video was shot in Washington State, not Ohio. [Cryptomundo, August 28, 2012.] Finally, on November 22, a driver traveling on Route 11 between Leetonia and Lisbon saw a light-brown Sasquatch cross the road and step over a guardrail before vanishing into the forest. ["Bigfoot Sighting in Lisbon, Ohio," *The Bigfoot Field Reporter*, http:// bigfootfieldreporter.com/wordpress/2012/12/03/bigfoot-sighting-in-lisbon-ohio.]

As this book went to press, three reports had been received for 2013. On March 14, while driving east on Route 90 in Ashtabula County, a motorist sighted a broad-shouldered biped 9 to 11 feet tall, covered with brownish-gray hair. [BFRO #40360.] Six days later, barking dogs alerted a homeowner outside Marengo, in Morrow County, to "something big" moving along the tree line near her rural home. [BFRO #40580.] In July, another video surfaced online, this one purporting to show a Sasquatch seen at Salt Fork State Park on July 3. The jerky 26-second clip, shot in near-total darkness, reveals a rather unconvincing creature peering around the corner of some nondescript structure, perhaps a portable toilet, before the photographer flees. ["Bigfoot Sighting — Salt Fork State Park, Ohio (July 3, 2013)," Community Reviewed.net, http:// communityreviewed.net/bigfoot-sighting-salt-fork-state-park-ohio-july-3-2013.]

Dates Unknown

Logic dictates that meeting Sasquatch in the wild should make a lasting impression, yet 10 reports from Ohio have no dates to offer. The first is all the more remarkable, describing how a Coshocton County mushroom hunter found "the remains of an arm. The arm resembled a human arm except it was very large and the skin was covered in thick dark hair. The fingers also had claws growing out of the fingers." The witness allegedly called "a specialist" to study the relic, and after examining it and running tests, "he concluded the hair and bones could not have came from an ape, human, bear, or any other creature he knew. He also said it may very well be the best evidence of bigfoot ever found. I'm not sure what happened after this but from what I have heard, days later more specialists came to see the arm and said they were going to take it to do more tests. It has not been seen since."[112]

If that tale smacks of fantasy, the rest are more mundane: a "very vague" report of odd sounds outside Oregonia; reports of "gorilla noises" heard around Williamsburg; "strange howls and strange odor," again from Williamsburg; a claim of "aggressive behavior from Bigfoot type creatures" at Friendship; a Sasquatch seen "covered with berries" near Sharon; another spotted wading in the Cuyahoga River; a creature howling at campers near Cleveland; sightings logged "for decades" by a family at Minford; and the tale of a "hideous creature" seen by teenage campers near Kettering.[113]

Fact or fiction? While diehard skeptics treat all sightings with disdain, and even open-minded researchers cannot agree on definitions of "conclusive" evidence, only one thing is clear: the mystery endures.

Chapter 8

Species

Unknown

The cases we've reviewed so far do not exhaust Ohio's archive of peculiar entities. The strangest still await us, and the list begins with giants.

Buckeye Behemoths

In 1800, 3 years before Ohio joined the Union as the seventeenth state, Aaron Wright staked out a homestead beside Conneaut Creek, in present-day Ashtabula County. While tilling the soil, he discovered "graves distinguished by slight depressions in the surface of the earth disposed in straight rows, with intervening spaces or alleys," covering 4 acres. There were at least 2,000 plots, each containing "human bones, blackened with time, which on exposure to the air soon crumbled to dust." Historian Henry Howe, writing in 1847, described some of those skeletons as "belonging to men of gigantic structure."[1]

How gigantic, exactly? Stephen Peet, writing in 1878, reported that "Mr. Peleg Sweet, who was a man of large size and full features...in digging, came upon a skull and jaw, which were of such size that the skull would cover his head and the jaw could be easily slipped over his face, as though the head of a giant were enveloping his."[2]

That discovery was made in 1808. Four years later, Solomon Spaulding allegedly exhumed "some human bones, portions of giant skeletons, and various relics" in the same area. Spaulding described the skeletons as "taller on an average than I had ever seen in any nation, their bones were large limbs strait [sic] and shoulders broad." Today, some researchers believe Spaulding fabricated his discovery, plagiarizing details from Irish author Thomas Ashe's *Travels in America* (1808).[3]

Perhaps. But what should we make of later accounts describing giant skeletal remains?

In 1829, while building a hotel in Chesterville, workmen unearthed a large skeleton. Again, as in the case from 1808, the skull could fit easily over a male adult's head. Its jaw also contained more teeth than the normal human complement.[4]

In 1872, residents of Seneca Township discovered 3 skeletons "at the very least 8 feet tall...with bone structure proportional to their height." Each possessed a double row of teeth.[5]

Reports emerged from 2 widely-separated counties in 1883. In Marion, construction workers and highway crews found "hundreds of human

GIANT SKELETON

Found in Bed of Sand in Northwestern Ohio—Man Was Eight
Feet High.

Bowling Green, O., Aug. 14—While
excavating for sand for building on

---

skeletons, some of them of giant form," 8 feet or taller. In Brown County, "mastodonic" remains displayed "the high cheek bones, powerful jaws, and massive frames peculiar of the red man."[6]

A document dated March 3, 1880, records excavations on the farm of J.M. Baughman, in Brush Creek Township, where skeletons of men and women, 8 and 9 feet tall, had been found buried in pairs over the past decade.[7]

Later in 1880, Zanesville laborers reportedly found a skeleton "of enormous dimensions in a clay coffin, with a sandstone slab containing hieroglyphics."[8]

In 1881, Medina County workmen found "a jawbone of great size belonging to a human being, which contained 8 jaw-teeth in each side, of enormous size; and the teeth stood transversely in the jawbone. It would pass over any man's face with ease."[9]

In 1888, Toledo witnessed the discovery of 20 skeletons "with jaws and teeth twice as large as those of normal humans."[10]

Headlines in the 19th century report discovery of a giant skeleton in Ohio.
Credit: Author's collection

On May 5, 1892, the Ironton Register announced discovery of "a skeleton of a very large person, all double teeth, and sound, in a jaw bone that would go over the jaw with the flesh on, of a large man."[11]

Toledo produced another score of skeletons "twice as large as those of present day people" in 1895. These had been buried sitting upright, facing to the east.[12]

In 1897, a farmer at Jackson dug up a single giant skeleton. The following year, 8 skeletons — one over 7 feet tall — were found on South Bass Island in Lake Erie, near the U.S. Coast Guard lighthouse.[13]

On April 7, 1904, a Wisconsin newspaper filed the following report: "A giant skeleton of a man has been unearthed on the Woolverton farm, a short distance from Tippecanoe City [now Tipp City]. It measures 8 feet from the top of the head to the ankles, the feet being missing. The skull is large enough to fit as a helmet over the average man's head. This skeleton was one of 7 found buried in a circle, their feet being pointed toward the center. Crude implements were near."[14]

On January 28, 2010, the *Toledo Gazette* reprinted an article published "about a century ago," describing excavation of a basement in Tiffin. Workmen had exhumed "a mammoth skeleton" more than 7 feet tall.[15]

Downsized

Giants aside, Ohio witnesses also report their share of "little people," not to be confused with humans suffering from growth hormone deficiency. The first report describes an apparent "pygmy" graveyard, discovered at Coshocton in May 1835. As reported in the *American Journal of Science*, some 3,000 skeletons were unearthed there, many of them less than 4 feet, 6 inches tall. George Eberhart speculates that the wee ones were children or dismembered adults, but obliteration of the cemetery in the 19th century makes confirmation impossible.[16]

Two years later, *Gentlemen's Magazine* announced discovery of a similar burial ground at an unnamed riverside location in Ohio, revealing skeletons 3 to 4 feet tall. Jerome Clark dismisses that report as a hoax, but it might as easily be a recap of the 1835 discovery.[17]

Modern reports of living little people strike a distinctly paranormal tone. One day in 1930, an 8-year-old Cincinnati girl saw a "balloon-like object" airborne near her home, then found a 6-inch humanoid figure lying in the gutter. It had a triangular face, with pointed ears and slanting eyes, and wore tight-fitting garments. The girl picked it up, but the thing escaped and ducked out of sight when a neighbor arrived to investigate.[18]

Driving through Hamilton County's Winton Woods on the night of August 25, 1955, Bill Wallace and 3 teenage companions saw "a little man" 3 to 4 feet tall. They told police it had "large yellow eyes, a dark face, and a glowing body," wore "an odd garment," and brandished a "claw-like hand." One night later, several witnesses glimpsed a similar claw-handed creature in nearby Cheviot.[19]

On January 3, 1967, a dwarfish humanoid entered the Athens County courthouse, displaying "odd behavior" that included fascination with the workings of a ballpoint pen. Sparse descriptions include a mention of dark hair.[20]

One year later to the day, in Ashtabula, Emma Grimble caught 2 small greenish-yellow "men" rattling tenants' mailboxes at her boarding house with "suction hands and feet." They wore glistening metallic garments and fled at her approach.[21]

On August 24, 1970, two 5-foot-tall peculiarities approached 3 persons at a bus stop in Olmsted Falls, a Cleveland suburb. The pair wore "glowing orange suits" that left only their yellowish faces exposed, and they carried a disc-like object above their heads. Two hours later, a young neighbor saw an object "shaped like a huge bubble" descend and retrieve 2 small figures from a nearby site.[22]

In November 1973, a motorist on Ward's Corner Road, in Loveland, saw a gray biped with large red eyes in a roadside field. It was 3 to 4 feet tall and "floated" before "evaporating." Two days later, witness Don Brandenberg saw a UFO land in the same field.[23]

"Patricia N." and her 3 daughters were driving through Mariemont on July 26, 1974, when they saw a weird pedestrian approaching. He was 5 feet tall, bald and bearded, without discernible features, walking with "a forward lunge" that produced "clicking" sounds. Shirtless to reveal a hairy chest, the walker wore "dark trousers with no visible bottoms," which somehow bared feet like a pig's hooves.[24]

One night in March 1975, trucker Bob DeTorre returned to his home in Millersburg and found a figure stepping off the porch. His uninvited visitor was 5 feet tall, "big shouldered," with a head "large for its size" but no visible features. Frightened, DeTorre fled and returned with police, who found nothing.[25]

On December 1, 1996, 2 hunters met 3 "grays" on Leonard Road, 6 miles south of Bethel. The creatures had large heads with black, slanting eyes, and wore matching coveralls. When seen, they retreated to a nearby saucer-shaped craft that rose straight up and vanished overhead.[26]

One Sunday morning in May 2000, a "bizarre little man" with shaggy hair, long pointed ears, and "beaver-like teeth" allegedly surprised a woman in her garden, at some undisclosed location in Ohio. He wore something like bib overalls, appeared to be collecting soil, and ignored the

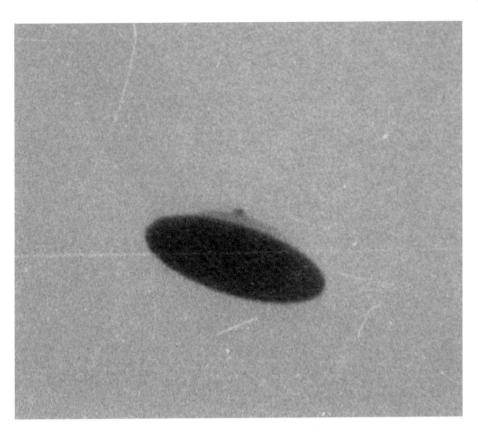

witness until she spoke. That startled him, and he ran into some nearby woods. Pursing him, the woman saw "a tiny disk-shaped object" soar aloft and vanish.[27]

On January 21, 2006, a resident of Fairborn saw a 3-foot-tall figure walking around his backyard. Frightened, he hid in his basement, then left for a friend's house, noting "a large diamond shaped light" shining in woods along New Trebien Road. Next morning, the same small trespasser appeared in his yard, prompting the witness to flee his home.[28]

Unidentified flying objects are linked to some Ohio "little people" sightings.
Credit: Author's collection

Varmints Galore

Historically, Americans — particularly in the Midwest and South — have used "varmint" as a generic term for any peculiar or unidentified creature. And Ohio has no shortage of varmints at large.

On December 31, 1884, newspapers reported sightings of "a strange wild animal" around Glenford. Witnesses compared it to "a panther, a lynx, a hyena, a bear, and dear knows what other names." All agreed that the elusive beast was "not a pleasant looking customer."[29]

On July 10, 1909, a "large and strange animal" frightened farmers south of Coshocton. They first suspected an escaped leopard, but on closer inspection of the creature found it to be "a huge dog, the like of which has never been seen in this vicinity," possessing "a massive body striped with dark and light brown." Wounded by gunshots, it escaped. Something like it appeared near Delphos in July 1910, where witness Isaac Good pronounced it a hyena (family *Hyaenidae*).[30]

Ohio witnesses described creatures resembling hyenas in the late 19th and early 20th centuries.
Credit: U.S. Fish & Wildlife Service

Ronan Coghlan reports that a creature "the size of a dozen cats" appeared in the backyard garden of a Columbus home, sometime in 1938. It was gray with yellow stripes and "possibly feline." No further information is available.[31]

Residents of Lafayette were plagued throughout the 1950s by a nocturnal prowler that "cried like a baby and screamed like a woman." Dallas Yoakam and his wife first heard the beast in 1950. Two years later, members of the same family lost a dog to the creature, while hunting raccoons at night. The hound was mangled, with a broken neck. Several other dogs were killed before the predator went on hiatus — then returned to shriek again in November 1956.[32]

Buckeye researcher Ron Schaffner shared a report from Laurelville in June 2002, involving "a cat that looks like a monkey." The unnamed witness claimed multiple sightings since 1993. The beast had "this big tail that curled on it's back, but it had a face like a panther, but it was so skinny, and when it leaped to run it had big paws like a cat....[I]t was jumping from one tree to another, and it leaped to the ground to run away." The witness noted that "we see lynx all the time where we live" — which would shock state experts who consider them extinct — and she insists the "cat/monkey" is something else. Schaffner noted in passing that the story "sounds similar to the 1997 Adams County report," but he supplied no further details on that case.[33]

Two witnesses en route to West Virginia saw a strange creature outside Marietta on December 11, 2003. As summarized by researcher Albert Rosales, it "looked like a strange mix between a deer and a bear. It stood about six and a half feet high in total. It had very long, extremely thin legs that looked almost unstable and its entire torso, neck and head was covered in very long black fur." Bare legs descended into grass that hid the beast's feet, but the witnesses noted large red eyes and a long snout with a "cat-like nose."[34]

Late on the night of March 1, 2006, a driver passing through Trumbull County saw a "beautiful" gray-and-white quadruped with "a white wolf-like face" at roadside. Before it fled into the woods, he estimated it stood 3 feet tall and measured 6 feet long, excluding its "very bushy tail." The witness thought its soulful eyes "looked inside of him."[35]

Two months later, central Ohio produced a rash of mysterious sightings. On May 6, Bob Lombardo of Lewis Center saw a beast with an "awkward stride" emerge from woods near his home. It was lean, quick, and its tail dragged on the ground. More sightings followed, from Pataskala and suburbs north of Columbus. Farmer John Kaminsky saw something cross the Millersport Road. "It was sleek, quick, and the color was gray and black," he explained. "It was different. I've seen fox. I've seen coyote. I've seen every kind of animal. I'm nearly 70. I've been around, but I've never seen an animal look like that."[36]

Ronan Coghlan relates the case of Ricky Hamilton, a Gallipolis resident who reported his encounter with a strange creature in 2006 (although it occurred "a few years previously"). The animal had a cat-like head, was the size of an opossum and walked with that marsupial's characteristic gait, while displaying rough hide like an armadillo's. Both opossums (family *Didelphidae*) and armadillos (family *Dasypodidae*) have long snouts, bearing no resemblance to a cat's face. An opossum suffering from hair loss might vaguely resemble an armadillo. Meanwhile, armadillos have expanded their normal southern range, with confirmed modern habitats including southern Missouri, Illinois, and Indiana, western Kentucky, through Kansas to southern Nebraska.[37]

April 2007 brought reports of "mysterious creatures" roaming the woods of Geauga County's Chester Township, described by police sergeant Debbie Davis as "half deer, half ram." Published photographs revealed goat-like creatures, while DNR spokesman Allen Lea declared, "We're not exactly sure what they are. But they're definitely not a native species. They're not where they belong." Chester Police Chief Mark Purchase shied away from sounding an alarm. "We're not looking to run them out," he said. "But we would like to know what they are."[38]

Warts and All

Ohio's best-known cryptid is the Loveland Frog. The story spans 6 decades, and it still has "legs," inspiring controversy to the present day.

Robert Hunicutt was driving through Loveland at 3:30 a.m. on May 25, 1955, when his headlights illuminated 3 diminutive figures beneath a bridge spanning the Little Miami River. They were roughly 3 feet tall, gray-skinned, with wide lipless mouths, and "corrugations rather than hair on their heads." Each had a "lopsided" chest, largest on the right. One held "something like a rod or chain" overhead, crackling with sparks. Hunicutt stopped to watch them for several minutes, noting a smell "like fresh-cut alfalfa, with a trace of almonds."[39]

Two months later, Loveland residents Emily Mangone and her husband woke to sounds of their dog barking and a swampy odor. Stepping outside with a neighbor, they saw a 3-foot-tall figure "entirely covered with twigs or foliage." It vanished when they turned on yard lights, then reappeared when the lights were shut off.[40]

Craig Woolheater, writing in 2006, suggested that Hunicutt's sighting, at least, may have been "spurred on" by the horror film *Creature from the Black Lagoon*, released in March 1954, about a man-sized bipedal reptile

inhabiting the Amazon River. That case cannot be proved today, nor did he mention the Mangone report.[41]

At 1:00 a.m., on March 3, 1972, an unidentified Loveland policeman met something he first took for a dog, on Riverside Road. Drawing closer, he saw the creature stand upright and leap over a guard rail, scrambling down a slope into the Little Miami. He described it as 3 to 5 feet tall, weighing 50 to 75 pounds, with a froglike face and "leathery textured" skin. His sketch depicts a biped with apparent webbed hands and feet, a ridge down its back, and a smile on its face. The officer reported his sighting and returned with a partner 2 hours later, finding "evidence of something that had scraped the embankment into the river."[42]

The Little Miami River at Loveland.
Credit: U.S. Geological Survey

Did a movie monster inspire sightings of the "Loveland frog"?
Credit: Author's collection

Opposite page:
A whimsical model of the
"Loveland frog."
Credit: Author's collection

Loveland still celebrates its
famous cryptid sightings.
Credit: Author's collection

Two weeks later, driving near the same spot on Riverside Road, Officer Mark Mathews had a sighting of his own and stopped to observe the creature. According to Ron Schaffner, "As he opened the car door, it made a noise which caused this thing to raise up in a crouch position, like a defensive lineman. The creature began to half-walk and half-hobble over to the guardrail. However, this time the creature lifted its leg over the railing. It kept its eyes on [Mathews] with a funny smirk on its face." Mathews fired a shot at the beast, but missed.[43]

Decades later, Mathews told a very different story to Craig Woolheater, writing:

> There is absolutely nothing to the incident that relates to "monsters" or the "paranormal." This entire thing has been habitually blown out of proportion....It was and is no "monster." It was not leathery or [had] wet matted fur. It was not 3-5 feet tall. It did not stand erect. The animal I saw was obviously some type of lizard that someone had as a pet that either got too large for its aquarium, escaped by accident, or they simply got tired of it. It was less than 3 feet in length, ran across the road and was probably blinded by my headlights. It presented no aggressive action." Mathews fired at the creature in hope that a specimen would vindicate his fellow officers, but it escaped.[44]

Wikipedia's article on the Loveland Frog asserts that a local farmer saw the creature pedaling a bicycle later in March 1972, but no other source confirms that strange report. Seven years would pass before Hollywood special-effects put Kermit the Frog aboard a bike in *The Muppet Movie*.[45]

While Loveland's Chamber of Commerce sponsors an annual Loveland Frog Festival at Nisbet Park, sporadic "frog" sightings continue. In September 1999, an anonymous witness reported seeing "a big green thing" splashing in the Little Miami, while he and a friend were drinking 40-ounce bottles of malt liquor at 3 a.m.[46]

On July 4, 2002, Jude Tillery and friend "Johnny H." were camped beside the Little Miami, drinking tequila "like madmen," when "a big frog lookin' dude" emerged from the river and raided their food supply, gobbling up Cheez Whiz before it retreated. The liquor—and Tillery's claim that Johnny sprouted "a lot of warts" within a week of the incident—strongly suggest a hoax.[47]

THE PLAIN DEALER, WEDNESDAY, APRIL 24, 1968

'Werewolf' Is Hunted by Teens Near Zoo

Armed with flashlights and 50 feet of plastic clothesline, four West Siders and a Parma teen-ager last night were trying to snare a werewolf in a woods near the Cleveland Zoo.

"It's eight feet tall and covered with hair," said the Parma youth, William Schwark, 17, of 5814 Bradley Avenue. "I chased it Monday night and it knocked me down a slope."

"It's a big black thing and it grabbed my buddy, Ron, by the shoulder, ripped his jacket and shirt and left big scratches on his shoulder," said Schwark's cousin, Dale, 16, of 3028 Sackett Avenue S.W.

Other werewolf hunters last night were the teen-agers with the plastic clothesline, Richard Sustersic, 15, of 2518 Marvin Avenue S.W., and John Juhas, 16, of 3351 W. 32d Street.

They haven't seen the werewolf but they contend they want to capture it and deliver it to the Second Police District. There's a certain amount of skepticism at police headquarers about the werewolf.

THE WEREWOLF hunters met The Plain Dealer at Stone's Open Grill, 3312 W. 25th Street, a restaurant they fancy for its food, jukebox and waitresses.

Mrs. Grace Lewis, the restaurant manager, of 1808 W. 54th Street, has a theory about the werewolf. She thinks it is "the monster of Riverside Cemetery. I've seen him myself. He's a big hairy man weighing 400 pounds who's been living like Tarzan for 25 years. I-71 destroyed his tunnel home back of the cemetery and he's been displaced to the woods back of the zoo."

Patrolman Sam Stimmel of the Second District was just as skeptical of the Riverside Cemetery "monster" as he

was of the Zoo woods Werewolf.

BUT THE werewolf hunters took Stimmel and The Plain Dealer to the woods. They showed a sapling they believe was broken by the werewolf as he chased Ron and Schwark. Bill Schwark had a white sheet with burn marks on it, a red flannel blanket and two white feathers.

Schwark contended the blanket and sheet were part of the werewolf's costume. The white feathers were all that remained of the werewolf's chicken dinner.

The Plain Dealer left the

werewolf hunters as the moon rose over the Zoo deerpens. A white-haired housewife asked what all the excitement was about.

"We're looking for a monster. Have you seen any in the woods there?"

"The only monsters I've seen," said the housewife, "are the teen-agers."

FOILED—Werewolf hunters, from left, Dale Schwark, William Schwark, Richard Sustersic and John Juhas.

Plain Dealer photo (Michael J. Zaremba)

Going to the Dogs

All cultures have legends of shape-shifting humans, with lycanthropes (werewolves) the best-known example. European immigrants brought classic werewolf tales to North America, while modern sightings supplement them with reports of savage hybrid "dogmen."

July and August 1972 brought a flurry of werewolf sightings from Toledo and Defiance, separated by 45 miles. Witnesses described a biped 6 to 8 feet tall, that looked "human, with an oversized, wolflike head and an elongated nose." It had "huge hairy feet, fangs, and ran from side to side, like a caveman in the movies." After it clubbed a railroad worker with a 2x4 in Defiance, Police Chief Donald Breckler told reporters, "We don't know what to think, but now we're taking it seriously."[48]

This "werewolf" article actually refers to 1968 Bigfoot sighting (see Chapter 7).
Credit: Author's collection

The action shifted farther south, to Montgomery County, in October 1972. Ed Miller and his wife were driving from Carlisle to Germantown, searching for their car's lost license plate, when they saw a black bipedal creature running in a nearby field. Mrs. Miller told the *Middletown Journal*, "It turned and came at us, and then it crouched down and was almost crawling. I screamed for my husband to take me home. I was scared to death." Three young friends heard their story and rushed to the site, observing the same beast, then the Millers returned for another look. "But we still couldn't get a close look at it," Mrs. Miller said. "It would start to run toward the car, standing up, then it would crouch down and hide in the weeds. And it howled at us, a loud snarling, hissing sound."[49]

Carlisle residents Gary Moore and his wife saw the beast after nightfall, vaguely describing it as black, "wide," and hairy, with huge eyes that "glowed like fluorescence in the light from the car." Both agreed that it was not a man in costume.[50]

Linda Godfrey, author of 5 books on dogmen and werewolves since 2003, reports an Ohio fisherman's sighting of "an extremely hairy person hunched over behind a bush" at some undisclosed location, in 2004. Before fleeing, the witness noted that its visage resembled a "mix between a dog's and a human's face."[51]

In August 2005, witness "Scott" phoned the *Coast to Coast AM* late-night radio talk show, relating his Ohio sighting of a bipedal monster with a "huge dog head" and legs "bent back" like a dog's. He compared it to werewolves depicted in the film *Van Helsing*, released in May 2004. Scott suggested that the beast might be responsible for eerie screams recorded at Liberty around the time of his sighting.[52]

On November 1, 2006, the *Delphos Herald* published a story unearthing early tales describing werewolf sightings around St. John's Resurrection Cemetery. Reporter Craig Adkins speculated that the stories were spawned by sightings of actual wolves, officially extirpated from Ohio by 1850.[53]

Hollywood tackles the "Dogman."
Credit: Author's collection

Hop to It!

We've all seen kangaroos (family *Macropodidae*), if not in person, then in films or photographs. We all know that they're native to Australia and New Guinea, nothing you should normally encounter running wild in North America. And yet...

In January 1949, bus driver Louis Staub spotted a peculiar creature hopping through Grove City, a Columbus suburb. He described it as "about 5½ feet high, hairy, and brownish in color. It had a long pointed head. It leaped a barbed wire fence and disappeared. It resembled a kangaroo, but it appeared to jump on all fours. I'm certain it wasn't a deer." Loren Coleman writes that some other "monster" was seen in Grove City around the same time, but provides no details.[54]

Late in May 1968, a motorist driving on State Route 63 near Monroe reported another kangaroo at large. Officer James Patrick of the Ohio State Highway Patrol responded and radioed back: "The thing hopped right across the road in front of my cruiser. It sure looked like a kangaroo to me." He thought it was headed toward Lebanon.[55]

Ed Maruska, director of the Cincinnati Zoo, disagreed without bothering to investigate. "I doubt there's a kangaroo around here on the loose," he said. "We had a kangaroo story about 2 years ago. Never found one. Down the years we've chased after reported black leopards, panthers, and even a polar bear. Anyway, anyone seeing the kangaroo, which I doubt exists, should try to keep it in sight and call the zoo."[56]

On August 18, 2004, Rick Schreiber reported 2 kangaroos grazing in the backyard of his home in Fairfield, a Cincinnati suburb. One fled before Animal Control Officer Chuck Geurin arrived to catch the other — which proved to be a wallaby, a smaller macropod related to kangaroos. While Guerin opined that, "He's definitely been a pet," searchers beat the bushes in vain for the wallaby's companion. Owner Frank Rosen reclaimed "Wally," but no follow-up reports were published on the second missing animal.[57]

While roaming pets may explain Buckeye kangaroo sightings, authors Loren Coleman and Mark Hall propose an alternate solution: "devil monkeys"! Witnesses describe these hypothetical primates as large, with protruding muzzles like those of baboons (genus *Papio*), with hind legs larger than their forefeet, and long (sometimes hairless) tails. Standing erect, such creatures might be misidentified as kangaroos or wallabies.[58]

Oddly, the lone suspected sighting of a devil monkey in Ohio does not match the prototype. On June 26, 1997, Debbie Cross saw a strange creature prowling around her home outside Dunkinsville, near the

Shawnee State Forest. "It was about 3 to 4 feet tall and gray in color," she said. "It had large, dark eyes and rounded ears extended above the head. It had *real long arms and a short tail.* It made a gurgling sound. From the available light, the animal appeared to have hair or fur all over its body about 1½ inches long."[59] (Emphasis added.)

A baboon, perhaps. But it bore no resemblance to a kangaroo.

Wallabies are smaller relatives of kangaroos.
Credit: U.S. Fish & Wildlife Service

Melon Heads

Stranger than meandering marsupials are tales of Buckeye "melon heads" — strange humanoids with bulbous skulls, reported chiefly from the neighborhood of Kirtland and Geauga County's Chardon Township. Described in campfire stories spanning half a century, these peculiar creatures have inspired a recent horror movie, *Legend of the Melonheads* (2010).[60]

www.laugh-at-the-law.com

The root of melon head mythology is a tale reminiscent of Frankenstein. A certain Dr. Crow (or Kroh) allegedly performed bizarre experiments on children suffering from hydrocephalus (water on the brain), producing monsters who eventually turned on him, then roamed at large to frighten or cannibalize random victims. One blogger online claims to document Dr. Crow's work from a local newspaper, the *West Geauga Sun*, but fails to cite a date or any other details.[61] While nearly all the tales of melon heads are third- or fourth-hand hearsay, 2 claim to be eyewitness accounts.

At 11 p.m., on July 9, 1978, while walking along railroad tracks near Butler, 2 young men met a 7-foot-tall humanoid figure with "a huge round head" and glowing red eyes, making an "unusual growling noise." They fled the area at once.[62]

On October 5, 2001, while riding with 3 relatives on Chillicothe Road in Chardon, witness "Tony" saw a melon-headed figure keeping pace with their car, at 45 miles per hour. He writes, "It looked about the same height as me (5 feet, 7 inches) and was wearing ripped-up brown pants held together by what looked like corn husk. It wore a white shirt with brown and red stains all over it. (I'm hoping the red stains weren't blood.) Its head was a very light brown tint with 2 holes in the sides that I think were ears. Its head was swelled up, and its eyes were very big. Just as we turned a curve, it jumped into the woods."[63]

An advertisement for *Legend of the Melonheads*.
Credit: Author's collection

Uninvited

Bizarre home invaders have pestered Ohio residents since August 1980, when a couple living at an undisclosed location woke to find a faceless, 4-foot-tall stranger in their bedroom. The visitor wore "a long flowing dress, with long grayish white hair to the floor; both hair and dress were blowing as if in breeze." Oddly, it left the witnesses with "a feeling of peace" as it dematerialized.[64]

On multiple occasions during 1982, a Euclid couple found their 10-year-old son sleeping outside their bedroom, refusing to enter his own. After several such incidents, the parents checked his room and found "a bird-like creature with big red eyes" sitting on the boy's headboard. It glared at them, then flew through a closed window and disappeared.[65]

In summer 1988, a child in Wellington woke to find himself paralyzed in bed, flanked by 2 "short wide figures" wearing hoods. The taller of them had large black eyes and strained its neck toward him, mouth opening, whereupon he was able to leap out of bed and the figures vanished.[66]

Five years later, a witness sleeping at his aunt's house, location undisclosed, woke to find "2 small bluish impish creatures" standing by the sofa where he lay. He bolted from the room, and they were gone when he returned.[67]

October 1994 produced our next report from another unrevealed location. The witness woke to find 3 entities at the foot of her bed, ranging from 3 to 4 feet tall. The shortest of them told her, telepathically, "Don't be afraid." After they disappeared, she "vaguely remembered the entities presenting her with a child and telling her that it was hers."[68]

A Dayton resident woke at 10 a.m. on May 5, 1995, to see a big-headed humanoid figure with small black eyes standing nearby. As she described it, "It had large ears and no obvious reproductive organs. The body seemed to consist of small veins, and larger ones, with nothing solid beneath them. It was brownish in color, possibly 'cloaking' itself." A small white object spun nearby, in mid-air, emitting flashes of light before it and the visitor vanished.[69]

Summer 1999 brought 2 sightings from a single witness at an undisclosed location. On the first occasion, he met "a small white creature with long arms, a fat stomach, and short legs" in his kitchen. A few weeks later, the same thing surprised him as he left the bathroom, rushing past before it disappeared.[70]

On December 7, 1999, a witness was listening to music in his home (location unknown) when a "dark figure" stepped from a closet and passed through the wall into another room. When he followed, it had disappeared.[71]

Finally, outside Cleveland, our last witness woke at midnight on March 11, 2003, to find 4 dark-gray, scaly-skinned figures standing over him. He reached for a gun in a nightstand, but lay frozen as one of the prowlers aimed a humming device at his head. Next, he remembered lying on a gurney, surrounded by 7 silent humanoids who probed his nose, mouth, and genitals. He woke sometime later, noting that his penis hurt and "appeared larger than normal."[72]

From Beyond?

If some of those cases suggest extraterrestrial contact, others from Ohio are more explicit. Two witnesses were berry-picking near Gallipolis, in 1912, when they saw "a dark cloud-like object" descend to treetop level. Turning to leave, they found a figure walking parallel to them, described as "dark in color with wide shoulders, a large bulky head, and no visible neck." The woman screamed, eliciting a snarl from their stalker before they escaped.[73]

One day in 1966, a Gallipolis farmer found several of her cattle killed and mutilated in bizarre fashion. Soon afterward, at night, she heard a commotion outside her home and grabbed a shotgun, confronting several tall "men" in white overalls. They fled on foot at high speed, "easily jumping" over fences to elude her.[74]

On March 12, 1967, while returning home from church in Letart Falls at 11:30 p.m., 2 witnesses saw "a huge white figure" in the road. It had long hair and was clearly visible in their headlights before it "shot up and disappeared." The witnesses assumed it was an "angel."[75]

West Akron resident Dollie Hansen was expecting a visit from aliens in August 1969, looking forward to a space flight they had promised her. At 2 a.m., on August 8, she answered a knock at her door to find "a superbly built young woman with deep chestnut hair but no features on her face." The caller led her to a car "wrapped in gray mist," occupied by 2 men, which conveyed her to a waiting UFO. Around the same time, a local youth reported taking a spaceship ride under similar circumstances.[76]

Our next witness was feeding rabbits at his home near Alum Creek, when he saw a humanoid figure clad in a black uniform with a silver belt. It's large head "emitted a yellow glow," while its limbs moved "with rhythm." The thing escaped when he ran to fetch his parents, but a neighbor reported strange lights over a nearby field, where a large oval depression appeared in tall grass.[77]

In Albany, on October 16, 1973, a woman saw a "ghost like" figure floating 50 feet above the ground, near a bright-white object 20 feet in diameter. The figure was 4 feet tall and resembled a person "draped in a close fitting sheet." Later, she saw a "little blue green thing" with stubby arms and "spiky things at the top and sides of the head," less than 3 feet tall, peering into her home.[78]

An unidentified man was driving near Whitehouse on State Route 64, at 12:15 a.m., on April 10, 1974, when his car suddenly died. Another car stopped behind him, and its driver — normal in appearance, with gray hair — engaged the witness in an odd conversation, urging the stranded motorist to "save" his marriage. While speaking, he used some hand-held implement to "dematerialize" a small stone, then left, whereupon the stalled car started up again.[79]

Jackie Booth of Avon Lake reported several UFO sightings between June and July 1974. On July 17, she found two gray-skinned visitors on her doorstep. They were 5 feet tall, had large heads, flat on top, with glowing wide-set eyes, lipless mouths, and long arms. They entered and engaged in telepathic conversation, during which Booth "felt my thoughts leave my head."[80]

On September 27, 1977, several children in Bellbrook reported a "large entity" floating over a schoolyard fence. Days later, the same witnesses claimed a UFO sighting.[81]

Driving through downtown Cincinnati at 1:18 a.m., on May 23, 1978, a woman saw a bald man with no facial features except slit-like eyes moving toward her car. The figure was 5 feet, 6 inches tall, wearing a black cape and "full-length gloves." The witness sped away.[82]

During summer 1980, while some residents of West Jefferson reported Bigfoot sightings (see Chapter 7), another met "something out of mythology." The glowing red figure resembled a centaur, half man and half horse, with "a pointed head and ears, fiery slanted eyes, a beard, and skinny wings." Crossing the witness's yard, it left cloven hoof prints behind.[83]

Late on June 28, 1981, members of a farming family at Rome saw "black forms" moving on their property. They approached, armed with shotguns, and fired repeatedly at flitting shapes with luminous red eyes, apparently wounding one before they ran out of shells and retreated. Later, the witnesses found 3-toed tracks and "ground disturbances" at the site of the skirmish.[84]

In March 1991, a youth playing basketball at his home (location undisclosed) saw a short figure with huge eyes in a "tremendously large head," dressed in a shimmering silver costume, peering at him from behind a tree. As he watched, it "suddenly glowed and vanished into thin air."[85]

Late in May 2004, witness "Bob" and a friend were walking home from a pool hall in Norwood, when they saw a man standing in an alley at 1:30 a.m. They watched the "crazy" stranger wave some object over an electric meter on the nearby wall, then walk into the wall and disappear.[86]

At 10 p.m., on June 23, 2004, a resident of Newton Falls saw 3 figures "made out of light" in her yard. They were "almost human-like in appearance, but with body appendages way out of proportion to the rest of the body," while the light that emanated from them changed from blue to green, then gray, finally fading into "a silvery trail" as they vanished.[87]

At 2 a.m., on March 5, 2006, while approaching their home in St. Louisville, a couple named Callis saw a pink, "skeletal" figure standing at the roadside. It was 6 feet tall, "hunched over with hands pulled up in a fetal position," but it fled with surprising speed as they approached. Later, they reported military helicopters circling the area.[88]

Two months later, on May 3, another 2 a.m. sighting occurred on Purity Road in Newark. Three witnesses saw a thin, pink 6-foot creature running swiftly along the road, "with its arms pulled up like one would if they were hopping like a bunny." They concluded that "it wasn't human but it was not an animal."[89]

While waiting with her daughters for their school bus, near West Alexandria, a farmer's wife felt her car begin to bounce, accompanied by a deafening "vacuum-type" sound, before an "arm" started pounding the left-rear passenger's window. Turning, the woman saw 2 "large yellow-cinnamon phosphorescent eyes" watching the car from woods 100 feet away.[90]

Between November 11 and 14, 2007, a "bizarre bluish amorphous entity" made several appearances in Parma, photographed on one occasion by a gas station's security camera. Some observers speculated that it was an "angel," while others claimed the filling station stood on an Indian burial ground.[91]

Finally, at 4:30 a.m., on June 12, 2009, a sleepless resident of Thornville saw a "human-like invisible creature" materialize from thin air in her yard, moving "faster than a human could walk" for some 30 feet, before it vanished again. How she could see an invisible creature remains unexplained, but she compared it to the title creatures from the *Predator* film franchise.[92]

Few of those sightings "make sense" in rational terms, and many strain credulity. I offer them for your consideration here as we complete our tour of monstrous and mysterious Ohio.

An 18th-century artist's depiction of centaurs in battle with humans.
Credit: Author's collection

End

Notes

Sources listed in the bibliography are abbreviated in notes below to save space. Abbreviations include:

BCBP: Brown County Bigfoot Project
BFRO: Bigfoot Field Researchers Organization
Bord, BC: Bord, The Bigfoot Casebook
Bord, UM20: Bord, Unexplained Mysteries of the 20th Century
COBR: Central Ohio Bigfoot Research
GCBRO: Gulf Coast Bigfoot Research Organization
HSR: Humanoid Sighting Reports
Ohio DNR: Ohio Department of Natural Resources
OMLW: Ohio Mountain Lion Watch
TSB: TriState Bigfoot.

Preface

1. "Ohio," Wikipedia.
2. "List of cities in Ohio," Wikipedia; Ohio Department of Natural Resources, http://www.ohiodnr.com.
3. Ohio DNR.

Chapter 1

1. Ohio DNR.
2. Ibid.
3. Ibid.
4. "Pacu," Wikipedia.
5. "Piranha," Wikipedia.
6. Ohio DNR.
7. WLWT-TV Channel 5 (Cincinnati), June 4, 2007.
8. WBNS-TV, Channel 10 (Columbus), August 11, 2011.
9. WKRC-TV, Channel 12 (Cincinnati), September 3, 2011.
10. "Alligator Effigy Mound," Wikipedia.
11. "Hooks Alligator in Ohio Pond, New York Times, July 7, 1935; USA Place Names; Bord, UM20, p. 381.
12. "Wayward alligator's no crock; it's the real thing," Akron Beacon Journal, January 30, 2003.
13. "Marsh monster captured in Ohio," Washington Times, September 30, 2004.
14. WKYC-TV, Channel 3 (Cleveland), October 3, 2006.
15. "Akron teen reels in an alligator from Summit Lake," Cleveland Plain Dealer, July 18, 2007.
16. "Athens police snap up toothy suspect," Columbus Dispatch, July 23, 2008.
17. "Chagrin River alligator eludes authorities," Columbus Dispatch, September 13, 2008.
18. "Grove City gator an easy capture," Columbus Dispatch, November 28, 2008.
19. "Teen catches what appears to be alligator in Summit Lake," Akron Beacon Journal, April 21, 2009.
20. "Ohio alligator causes a stir as onlookers throw meat, rocks," Galesburg Register-Mail, July 10, 2009.
21. "Alligator caught by police officer in Hamilton," Dayton Daily News, July 26, 2009.
22. "Dog finds alligator outside Near East Side business," Columbus Dispatch, June 17, 2010.
23. "Ohio Division of Wildlife kills wayward caiman crocodilian," Cleveland Plain Dealer, June 29, 2010.

24. "This is no croc! Florida gator in Summit Lake," *Akron Beacon Journal*, July 8, 2010.
25. "Deputy called on to kill gator," *Columbus Dispatch*, May 14, 2011.
26. "Alligator found on highway in Columbus, Ohio," NewsCraze, http://newscraze.net/?p=11126.
27. "Baby alligator rescued from Ohio sewer plant," *Columbus Dispatch*, September 30, 2011.
28. Ohio State Laws Governing Private Possession of Exotic Animals, Born Free USA, http://www.bornfreeusa.org/b4a2_exotic_animals_state.php?s=oh.
29. "Monitor lizard," Wikipedia.
30. "Nasty Nile monitors showing up in South Florida," *Fort Lauderdale Sun Sentinel*, July 5, 2011.
31. "Ohio man guns down giant lizard," *Washington* (PA) *Observer-Reporter*, February 27, 1984.
32. "Large monitor lizard sighted twice in Janesville," *Janesville Gazette*, September 29, 2010.
33. Ohio DNR.
34. Ibid.; "Hogzilla," Wikipedia; "Monster Pig," Wikipedia.
35. Ohio DNR.
36. *Creature Chronicles* No. 14, p. 3.
37. WCPO-TV, Channel 9 (Cincinnati), September 11, 2003.
38. WCMH-TV, Channel 4 (Columbus), September 23, 2005.
39. Ohio DNR.
40. Ibid.
41. "Phone camera verifies Ohio porcupine," *Toledo Blade*, January 24, 2006.
42. "Bobcats returning to Ohio," *Columbus Dispatch*, January 29, 2012.
43. "Wolf hunting," Wikipedia; "Hybrid wolves escape and roam parts of Ohio," *Cleveland Plain Dealer*, March 25, 2010; "Sandusky County man shoots wolf in Bellevue," WTOL-TV, Channel 11 (Toledo), March 20, 2010.
44. "Reports of unusual wildlife filed with police," *Dover Times-Reporter*, June 17, 2011; "Wolf sightings reported in Tuscawaras County," WTOV-TV, Channel 9 (Steubenville), July 18, 2011.
45. Ohio DNR; "Canada Lynx," Ohio History Central, http://www.ohiohistorycentral.org/entry.php?rec=1135; "The Canada Lynx," U.S. Fish & Wildlife Service, http://library.fws.gov/Pubs/lynx.pdf.
46. Arment, *Varmints*, pp. 500-1; "Species Profile: Canada Lynx," U.S. Fish & Wildlife Service, http://ecos.fws.gov/speciesProfile/profile/speciesProfile.action?spcode=A073; "Canada Lynx," Wikipedia.
47. Arment, *Varmints*, p. 501; OMLW.
48. Ohio DNR; "Increased sightings of bobcats in Ohio," Big Cat Rescue, http://bigcatrescue.blogspot.com/2009/03/increased-sightings-of-bobcats-in-ohio.html.
49. Big Cat Rescue.
50. "Snap of a shutter confirms bobcat sighting in Boston Heights," *Cleveland Plain Dealer*, September 25, 2010.
51. "Wildlife biologists verify more than 100 bobcat sightings in Ohio," WDTN-TV, Channel 2 (Dayton), February 10, 2011.

Chapter 2

1. Harry Miller, "The Cat Came Back," 1883.
2. Mountain Lion Foundation, http://mountainlion.org/Cougar_Timeline.asp; Bolgiano and Roberts, p. 19.
3. "Cougar," Wikipedia; "Florida panther count steady despite roadkill record," Scripps Howard News Service, May 19, 2010.
4. "Comprehensive List of Cougar/Black Panther Reports from 1960-Present," Eastern Puma Research Network, 2005.
5. Ibid.; Lutz and Lutz, pp. 31, 45.
6. "Cougar sightings pour in, but there's still no proof," *Canton Repository*, July 7, 2011.
7. Humanoid Sighting Reports, 1968; Coleman and Clark, p. 17.
8. Coleman and Clark, p. 18.
9. Ibid.
10. Bord, *Alien Animals*, p. 198.
11. William Reichling, "R&R Animal Trackers' Puma Research Project," EPRN News 23 (October 2005): 7.
12. Butz, pp. 211-12.
13. Arment and LaGrange.
14. BFRO #8406.
15. "Big cat," Wikipedia.
16. "Residents encounter mountain lion," *Martins Ferry Times Leader*, September 24, 2003.
17. "Rumors, sightings of big cat resurface," *Newark* (OH) *Advocate*, July 30, 2004.
18. "Couple finds large cat tracks on property," *Zanesville Times Recorder*, July 27, 2004; "Safety the focus with large cat on loose," *Zanesville Times Recorder*, August 3, 2004; "Sightings, attacks continue in hunt for large cat," *Zanesville Times Recorder*, August 14, 2004; "Big cat getting big attention," *Newark Advocate*, August 20, 2004.
19. "Large cat spotted in sheriff's backyard," *Zanesville Times Recorder*, September 1, 2004; "Trap set for big cat," *Zanesville Times Recorder*, September 2, 2004; "Another 'big cat' sighting reported," *Zanesville Times Recorder*, September 16, 2004; "Muskingum cat remains on loose," *Newark Advocate*, September 19, 2004.
20. "Zanesville visitor spots big cat," *Newark Advocate*, September 30, 2004.
21. "Neighbors cautious; some think 'big cat' was dog," *Zanesville Times Recorder*, October 1, 2004; "Hunters may have area's 'big cat' in their sights," *Zanesville Times Recorder*, October 27, 2004.
22. WTOL-TV, Channel 11 (Toledo), February 15, 2005.
23, WBNS-TV, Channel 10 (Columbus), December 11, 2005.
24. WCMH-TV, Channel 4 (Columbus), May 8, 2006.
25. Ibid., November 27, 2006.
26. "Big cat gives 'paws,'" *Wilmington* (OH) *News Journal*, January 13, 2007.
27. "Residents say they've seen big cat prowling near Lima," *Akron Beacon Journal*, June 6, 2008.
28. "Couple insist big cat prowling nearby," *Akron Beacon Journal*, August 6, 2008.

29. "Second sighting of possible big cat in Richfield village," *Akron Beacon Journal,* October 6, 2008.
30. Ibid.
31. Ibid.
32. Ibid.
33. "Possible sightings of big cats reported in Ohio," Maysville (OH) *Ledger Independent,* May 22, 2009.
34. "State game doesn't believe Salem mountain lion story true," *Salem* (OH) *News,* January 22, 2010.
35. OMLW.
36. WCMH-TV, Channel 4 (Columbus), May 4, 2010.
37. "Family tries to identify cat-like creature," Fremont (OH) *News-Messenger,* May 10, 2010; "Gibsonburg family spots possible mountain lion," Fremont *News-Messenger,* May 11, 2010.
38. "Police on prowl for big cat," Fremont *News-Messenger,* May 20, 2010; "Oak Harbor residents spot large feline," Fremont *News-Messenger,* May 21, 2010.
39. "More 'strange feline' sightings reported," Fremont *News-Messenger,* May 25, 2010.
40. "Mountain lion believed sighted near Georgetown," Maysville *Ledger Independent,* May 27, 2010.
41. OMLW.
42. Ibid.
43. Ibid.
44. Ibid.
45. Ibid.
46. Ibid.
47. Ibid.
48. "Big cat on the prowl?" Cambridge *Daily Jeffersonian,* March 8, 2011.
49. "Ohio mountain lion attacking livestock?" Cambridge *Daily Jeffersonian,* June 30, 2011.
50. "Cougar or house cat: What is it?" *Cleveland Plain Dealer,* June 26, 2011.
51. OMLW.
52. Ibid.
53. Ibid.
54. "Ohio mountain lion attacking livestock?" Cambridge *Daily Jeffersonian,* June 30, 2011.
55. OMLW.
56. Ibid.
57. Ibid.
58. Ibid.
59. "Mountain lion reported loose in Ohio," CNN, July 5, 2011; "Mountain lion scare closes Ohio park," *Sandusky Register,* July 6, 2011; "Cougar sightings pour in, but there's still no proof," *Canton Repository,* July 7, 2011; "Is this the cougar that's been prowling Stark?" *Canton Repository,* July 8, 2011; "It's a cougar, say couple who took photo, but others doubt it," *Canton Repository,* July 9, 2011.
60. OMLW.
61. Ibid.
62. "Cougar afoot in Tuscarawas County?" Dover *Times Reporter,* July 13, 2011.
63. "New cougar sightings reported; cat kills duck," Dover *Times Reporter,* July 14, 2011.
64. OMLW.
65. Ibid.
66. Ibid.
67. "Man attacked by mountain lion SE side of Canton, Ohio," YouTube, July 24, 2011,

http://www.youtube.com/
watch?v=dUIOtUbMFBg.
68. OMLW.
69. Ibid.
70. Ibid.
71. Ibid.
72. Ibid.
73. Ibid.
74. Ibid.
75. Ibid.
76. Ibid.
77. Ibid.
78. Ibid.
79. Ibid.
80. Ibid.
81. Ibid.
82. Ibid.
83. Ibid.
84. Ibid.
85. Ibid.
86. Ibid.
87. Ibid.
88. Ibid.
89. Ibid.
90. Ibid.
91. Ibid.
92. Ibid.
93. Mountain Lion Foundation.
94. Ibid.
95. Ibid.
96. Ibid.
97. Ibid.
98. Ibid.

Chapter 3

1. ABC News, October 19, 2011.
2. Ibid.; "Missing Zanesville monkey may carry herpes virus," *Pittsburgh Post-Gazette*, October 19, 2011.
3. "Black Panther," Wikipedia; "Jaguar," Wikipedia.
4. *New York Times*, January 20, 1877.
5. Coleman, p. 293.
6. Arment, *Varmints*, p. 502.
7. Ibid., p. 504.
8. Ibid., pp. 505-6; Coleman, p. 130.
9. Arment, *Varmints*, pp. 506-7; WNWO-TC, Channel 24 (Toledo), September 22, 2010.
10. Arment, *Varmints*, p. 507.
11. EPRN 2006 flier.
12. Arment, *Varmints*, p. 507.
13. Ibid., pp. 507-8.
14. Ibid., pp. 508-9.
15. Ibid., pp. 509-11.
16. *Cleveland Plain Dealer*, March 23, 2005.
17. Arment, *Varmints*, pp. 513-14.
18. Coleman, p. 109.
19. Arment, *Varmints*, p. 514,
20. Ibid., p. 515.
21. Ibid.; Clark and Coleman, pp. 209-17.
22. Eberhart, p. 176.
23. Ron Schaffner, "Phantom Panthers in Suburbia," *Fate* 38 (May 1985): 71-3.
24. *Cleveland Plain Dealer*, March 23, 2005.
25. Arment, *Varmints*, p. 516.
26. *Cleveland Plain Dealer*, March 23, 2005.
27. *Port Clinton News Herald*, May 4, 2004.
28. Ibid., June 16, 2004.
29. *Newark Advocate*, December 12 and 14, 2005; WCMH-TV, Channel 4 (Columbus), December 13, 2005.
30. Lima News, June 9, 2008.
31. Ibid.
32. Ibid.
33. *Dayton Daily News,* July 12, 2011.
34. OMLW.
35. Ibid.

36. *Dayton Daily News*, September 1, 2011.
37. OMLW.
38. *Strongsville Patch*, October 15, 2011.
39. *Dayton Daily News*, October 25 and 26, 2011.
40. *Pittsburgh Tribune-Review*, December 11, 2011.
41. OMLW.
42. Ibid.
43. Arment, *Varmints*, pp. 488-91.
44. Ibid., pp. 494-5.
45. Ibid., p. 498.
46. Ibid., p. 502.
47. Coleman, p. 131.
48. Ibid., p. 133.
49. Ibid., p. 295; Arment, *Varmints*, p. 515.
50. Coghlan, *Dictionary*, pp. 13-14; Coleman, p. 295.
51. Shuker, p. 168.
52. Coleman, p. 135; "North Olmsted, Ohio," Wikipedia.
53. Coleman, p. 135.
54. Ibid.
55. Ibid., pp. 143-4.
56. *Cincinnati Enquirer*, July 3 and 4, 2003; *Cincinnati Post*, July 3, 2003; *Dayton Daily News*, July 3, 2003.
57. WCMH, Channel 4 (Columbus), May 3, 4, 7, 10 and 13, 2004; WLWT, Channel 5 (Cincinnati), May 6, 2004.
58. *Newark Advocate*, May 14 and July 9, 2004; WCMH, Channel 4 (Columbus), June 25 and July 10, 2004; *Zanesville Times Recorder*, July 27, 2004.
59. *Newark Advocate*, November 6, 2004; *Coshocton Tribune*, November 17, 2004.
60. *Newark Advocate*, January 4, 2005.
61. *Columbus Dispatch*, January 28, 2007.
62. Coleman, p. 143.
63. Ibid.
64. *Medina Gazette*, April 6, 2001.
65. Arment, *Varmints*, pp. 501-2.
66. Ibid., p. 503.
67. Ibid., pp. 503-4.
68. Ibid., pp. 512-13; *Creature Chronicles* No. 6 (Spring 1983): 7.
69. Arment, *Varmints*, p. 515.
70. Coghlan, *Further Cryptozoology*, p. 131.
71. Cincinnati Enquirer, March 25, 2010.
72. *Newark Advocate*, July 22, 2010.
73. OMLW.
74. Ibid.
75. Arment, "North American Black Panthers," pp. 41-5.
76. "American lion," Wikipedia; Coleman, pp. 150-9.

Chapter 4

1. Mark Hall, "Sobering Sights of Pink Unknowns," *Wonders* (December 1992): 60-4.
2. Ohio DNR.
3. "Giant salamander," Wikipedia.
4. Sucik, p. 138-9.
5. Ibid.
6. "Monitor lizard," Wikipedia; "Megalania," Wikipedia.
7. Ohio DNR.
8. Ibid.
9. Ibid.; "Coral snake," Wikipedia.
10. Arment, "Corals and Kings," p. 44.
11. Ibid.
12. Ibid., pp. 44-5.
13. Ibid., p. 45.
14. Ibid., pp. 45-6.
15. Ibid., p. 46.

16. Ibid.
17. WCPO-TV, Channel 5 (Cincinnati), August 18, 2011.
18. Arment, *Boss Snakes*, p. 230.
19. Ibid., p. 231.
20. Ibid., pp. 231-4.
21. Ibid., pp. 234-5.
22. Ibid., pp. 235-8.
23. Ibid., p. 238.
24. Ibid., pp. 45, 239.
25. Ibid., p. 239.
26. Ibid.
27. Ibid., p. 240.
28. Ibid., pp. 240-1.
29. Ibid., pp. 241-2.
30. Ibid., p. 242.
31. Ibid., p. 246.
32. Ibid., p. 251; USA Place Names.
33. Arment, *Boss Snakes*, pp. 246-7.
34. Ibid., p. 247.
35. Ibid., pp. 246-7.
36. Clark, pp. 257-8.
37. Arment, *Boss Snakes*, p. 249.
38. Ibid.
39. Ibid., p. 250.
40. Ibid.
41. Ibid., pp. 250-1.
42. Ibid., p. 251.
43. Ibid., pp. 251-2.
44. Ibid., pp. 252-3.
45. Clark, p. 263.
46. Arment, *Boss Snakes*, pp. 253-4.
47. Ibid., p. 255.
48. Ibid.
49. Ibid., pp. 255-6.
50. Ibid., pp. 256-7.
51. Ibid., p. 257.
52. Ibid., p. 258.
53. Ibid.
54. Ibid., pp. 258-9.
55. Ibid., p. 259.
56. Ibid., pp. 259-60.
57. Ibid., p. 260.
58. Ibid., pp. 260-1.
59. Ibid., pp. 260-6.
60. Ibid., p. 266.
61. Ibid., pp. 267-70; Discover Peninsula, http://www.explorepeninsula.com/page.aspx?ID=100.
62. Arment, *Boss Snakes*, p. 271.
63. Ibid., p. 271.
64. Scioto Marsh, http://www.oocities.org/hly2oo1.
65. "Python reticulatus," Wikipedia.

Chapter 5

1. Ohio DNR; USA Place Names.
2. Albert Gatschet, "Water Monsters of American Aborigines," *Journal of American Folklore* 12 (1899): 255-60.
3. "Catfish," Wikipedia.
4. Coghlan, *Dictionary*, p. 89; Coleman, p. 93; *Independent Herald* (Oneida, TN), August 18, 2005; Cryptomundo, March 7, 2006.
5. *Creature Chronicles* No. 6, p. 7.
6. *Fort Wayne* (IN) *Journal*, August 11, 2006; *Louisville Courier-Journal*, April 16, 2009.
7. Ohio DNR.
8. "Kraken," Wikipedia.
9. The Northwest Ohio Phenomena Report, http://www.noprcentral.com/database.php?id=47; *Bryan* (Ohio) *Times*, July 25, 1994.
10. "Joe Roush's Sea Serpent," *Fate* 7 (March 1954): 10-11; USA Place Names.
11. Coghlan, *Dictionary*, p. 205.
12. USA Place Names.
13. *Columbus Citizen-Journal*, April 5, 1982.

14. Ohio DNR.
15. Ibid.; "Charles Mill Lake Monster," American Monsters, http://www.americanmonsters.com/site/2011/04/charles-mill-lake-monster-ohio-usa.
16. "Charles Mill Lake Monster"; BFRO #7206.
17. "Lake Erie," Wikipedia.
18. "Does a Sea Monster Haunt Lake Erie's Shores?" Newsvine, http://primarysources.newsvine.com/_news/2006/10/10/394874-does-a-sea-monster-haunt-lake-eries-shores; "Bessie (lake monster)," Wikipedia; "Northern Water Snake," Wikipedia.
19. "Bessie," Wikipedia; Eberhart, p. 511.
20. "Bessie," Wikipedia; Columbus Dispatch, July 7, 2003.
21. "Bessie," Wikipedia; Kirk, p. 144.
22. "Bessie," Wikipedia.
23. "Bessie," Unknown Explorers, http://www.unknownexplorers.com/bessie.php.
24. Ibid.
25. "Bessie," Wikipedia.
26. Schaffner, p. 35.
27. Ibid.
28. Ibid.
29. Ibid.
30. Ibid.
31. Ibid., pp. 35-6.
32. Ibid, p. 36.
33. Ibid.
34. Herdendorf; "Huron, Ohio," Dark Destinations, http://www.thecabinet.com/darkdestinations/location.php?sub_id=dark_destinations&letter=h&location_id=huron_ohio.
35. Schaffner, p. 35; Eberhart, p. 511.
36. "Huron, Ohio," Dark Destinations.
37. Schaffner, pp. 37-8.
38. Glen Kuban, "Lake Erie Sea Monster?" http://paleo.cc/paluxy/eriebaby.htm.
39. Ibid.
40. Ibid.
41. "Bessie," Wikipedia.
42. London (Ontario) Free Press, August 12, 2001.
43. "Esox," Wikipedia; "Snakehead (fish)," Wikipedia.
44. "Sturgeon," Wikipedia; "Bessie," Unknown Explorers.
45. Associated Press, August 19, 2006.

Chapter 6

1. Ohio DNR.
2. Keel, pp. 252-3.
3. Ibid., pp. 253-4.
4. "Teratornithidae," Wikipedia.
5. Coghlan, Dictionary, p. 57.
6. Ibid., p. 9; "The Gorge," Metro Parks, http://www.summitmetroparks.org/parksandtrails/gorge.aspx.
7. Keel, 245-52.
8. Ibid, p. 270.
9. Ibid., p. 272; Hall, Thunderbirds, p. 165.
10. Coghlan, Cryptosup, p. 14.
11. Ibid.
12. HSR.
13. Phantoms & Monsters, http://phantomsandmonsters.wetpaint.com/page/Tall+Dark+'Mothman'+Type+Entity+Reported+-+Stow,+Ohio.
14. Ibid.
15. Mothman Mystery, http://mothmanmystery.com/2011/05/

update-mothman-sighting-middletown-ohio/.
16. Hall, *Thunderbirds*, pp. 159-62.
17. William Connelly, *Wyandot Folklore* (Topeka: Crane, 1899), pp. 85-6.
18. Hall, *Thunderbirds*, p. 168.
19. Ibid.
20. "Owl," Wikipedia.
21. "Pterosaur," Wikipedia.
22. HSR.
23. Ibid.
24. Live Pterosaurs in America, http://www.livepterosaurs.com/inamerica/blog/?p=227.
25. Ibid.
26. Pterosaurs in the Bible, http://www.angelfire.com/mi/dinosaurs/flyingserpent.html.
27. Pterosaur Eyewitness, http://www.livingpterosaur.com/blog/2010/09/15/reports-of-pterosaurs-in-ohio.
28. Live Pterosaurs in America.
29. Coghlan, *Dictionary*, p. 84.

Chapter 7

1. Northeast Ohio Bigfoot, http://www.facebook.com/pages/Northeast-Ohio-Bigfoot/258793520841858?sk=wall.
2. Arment, *Historical*, p. 227.
3. Ibid., pp. 227-8.
4. Ibid., pp. 228-9.
5. Arment, *Historical*, pp. 229-30.
6. Murphy, pp. 60-1.
7. Arment, *Historical*, p. 230.
8. Ibid., pp. 230-1.
9. Ibid., pp. 231-2.
10. Murphy, pp. 57-8.
11. Arment, *Historical*, pp. 232-7,
12. Ibid., p. 238.
13. Ibid., pp. 239-47.
14. Ibid., pp. 248-54.
15. Murphy, p. 80.
16. Ibid., p. 63; Arment, *Historical*, p. 254.
17. Arment, *Historical*, p. 254.
18. BFRO #5333.
19. HSR.
20. Murphy, pp. 48, 75.
21. BFRO #4982.
22. Our Bigfoot, http://ourbigfoot.com/bigfoot_about_us.html; Cryptomundo, http://www.cryptomundo.com/bigfoot-report/ourbigfoot.
22. Murphy, p. 80; BFRO #8086.
23. BFRO #7425; Murphy, p. 75.
24. Bord, BC, p. 165; Murphy, p. 53.
26. BFRO #3651.
27. Bord, BC, p. 168.
28. Ibid; ; Murphy, pp. 75-6.
29. BFRO #7026.
30. Bord, BC, p. 71.
31. Ibid., p. 169.
32. COBR; HSR.
33. Murphy, p. 94.
34. GCBRO.
35. BFRO #7830.
36. Bord, BC, pp. 91-2.
37. Ibid., pp. 175-6; Murphy, p. 54.
38. BFRO #4953.
39. Murphy, pp. 76-9.
40. Bord, BC, p. 89.
41. Clark and Coleman, p. 112.
42. Murphy, p. 58.
43. Ibid., pp. 55, 92.
44. Ibid., p. 55; BFRO #4968.
45. BFRO #4307, 4983.
46. Murphy, pp. 54, 55, 63; BFRO #4959; GCBRO.
47. Murphy, pp. 55-6, 67, 76, 80; Bord, BC, p. 196.
48. BFRO #3385, 14223, 24435; Murphy, pp. 48, 56.

49. Murphy, pp. 72, 117, 138.
50. Ibid., pp. 72; Bord, BC, p. 208; BFRO #4837, 4966, 8494, 8587, 10862, 24435.
51. BFRO #374, 1625, 4556, 4970, 4975, 14223; Murphy, p. 51, 71-3; Bord, BC, p. 213-14.
52. COBR; BFRO #2450, 3293, 8836, 8944; GCBRO.
53. Bord, BC, p. 222; Murphy, pp. 62-3, 76-9; HSR.
54. BFRO #4484, 4977; *Canton Repository*, August 15, 2004; Murphy, pp. 80-3.
55. BFRO #3180, 4960, 4972, 7220, 7431.
56. Murphy, pp. 49, 52, 61, 64, 68, 83, 84; BFRO #6548, 8394, 8406.
57. Murphy, pp. 52, 68; BFRO #4955, 7220.
58. Murphy, pp. 64, 68, 92; BFRO #4762.
59. Murphy, pp. 49, 52, 64-5; BFRO #4306, 12220.
60. Murphy, pp. 65, 90; *Waukegan News Sun*, June 26, 1980.
61. Murphy, pp. 65, 91
62. Murphy, pp. 53, 64, 68-9; BFRO #4484, 7133, 7803.
63. Murphy, pp. 92-4; BFRO #322, 3301, 7940; GCBRO; HSR.
64. Murphy, pp. 47, 93-4; BFRO #322, 3920.
65. BFRO #1507, 4976; Murphy, p. 91.
66. Murphy, pp. 58-9, 65-6, 91-2.
67. BFRO #3352, 4731, 4956; Murphy, pp. 65, 69, 70; HSR.
68. Murphy, pp. 52-3, 55; HSR; GCBRO.
69. BFRO #841, 2696, 4306, 7220, 10421, 12597; GCBRO.
70. BFRO #4969, 4981, 5311, 12669.
71. Murphy, p. 59; GCBRO; BFRO #4073, 8236, 8406,

72. BFRO #5229, 12736; Murphy, p. 70; *Cleveland Plain Dealer*, February 2, 2003.
73. Murphy, p. 58; BCBP; BFRO #6062, 7832, 8017, 25961.
74. BFRO #3351, 4957, 5778, 14606; Murphy, p. 53.
75. Murphy, pp. 53, 62, 79, 84; BFRO #4310, 4952, 4962, 4980, 26997.
76. BFRO #878, 1018, 4982, 8406; Murphy, p. 84.
77. BFRO #7085, 4976.
78. BFRO #3380, 4200, 4982, 10925; COBR; *Liverpool Daily Post*, April 28, 2003; GCBRO.
79. Murphy, pp. 102-3; BFRO #5030, 10729.
80. GCBRO; Murphy, pp. 107-8; BFRO #1750, 4458; BCBP.
81. BFRO #359, 4202, 4961, 28820.
82. GCBRO; Murphy, pp. 49-51, 84, 94; BFRO #6804; BCBP.
83. BFRO #2850, 4982, 5259, 13882, 15885; Murphy, pp. 40, 49-50, 59-60, 90; Bigfoot Encounters, http://www.bigfootencounters.com/articles/buckeye.htm.
84. Murphy, p. 41, 51, 73-5; Don Keating email, February 17, 2002; BFRO #4974, 8042.
85. BFRO #3080, 3386, 4967, 5551; Murphy, pp. 51, 89-90, 140.
86. BFRO #3315, 3381, 4557, 4951, 5262, 7493; HSR.
87. Murphy, p. 47; BFRO #2902, 3589, 3686, 4950.
88. BFRO #378, 1751, 3533, 3767, 4558, 4973, 5267, 23125; GCBRO.
89. Don Keating emails, February 9 and July 22, 2002; BFRO #982, 2332, 4176, 4201, 4950, 11248; GCBRO.
90. BFRO #3350, 4555, 4964, 26011.

91. BFRO #4555, 4978, 5977, 7995, 25724; GCBRO.
92. BFRO #257, 7936; GCBRO.
93. BFRO #1117, 1755, 1756, 4299, 5013, 8778.
94. BFRO #1851, 3248, 3535, 5551.
95. BFRO #4672, 6620, 8006; Murphy, pp. 63-4; GCBRO.
96. BFRO #6900, 7973, 26709; GCBRO; Rich La Monica email, January 9, 2002.
97. GCBRO; COBR; Murphy, pp. 41-6.
98. BFRO #4409, 4498, 4659, 4760, 4762, 8785, 9537; Don Keating email, July 16, 2002; GCBRO.
99. BFRO #5076, 5406, 6045, 7932, 16489, 17388; Don Keating email, November 6, 2002.
100. BFRO #6313, 6330, 10330, 11946, 12157, 24141.
101. Murphy, p. 80; BFRO #6722, 6804, 7224, 7718, 15969.
102. BFRO #8446, 8450, 8843, 9022, 9042, 9129, 9188, 9281, 9766, 15430, 17317.
103. BCBP; BFRO #10766, 10863, 11771, 12157, 15088, 15876, 24356, 25715, 26369; GCBRO.
104. BFRO #2574, 15371, 15430; GCBRO; Searching for Bigfoot Inc., http://www.searchingforbigfoot.com/Ohio_Photos_May_2006.
105. BFRO #29018.
106. GCBRO; BFRO #23980, 29158; TSB #1091209; Reports of Sasquatch Sightings in Ohio, http://christineritter.hubpages.com/hub/Reports_of_Sasquatch_Sightings_in_Ohio.
107. BCBP; BFRO #25948, 25961, 26149, 26830, 27613; GCBRO; TSB #1011710, 1052210; YouTube, http://www.youtube.com/watch?v=b3a8pqBcdFg.
108. TSB #1052811, 1061111, 1081311.
109. BCBP; BFRO #27972, 28499, 28531, 28730, 28998; TSB #1100910, 1110710.
110. BFRO #28912, 30035, 30622; BCBP; TSB #1102211.
111. BCBP.
112. GCBRO.
113. TSB #1031911, 1090311, 1091711, 1101511, 1102310; Bigfoot Encounters, http://www.bigfootencounters.com/articles/buckeye.htm; "Bigfoot in Ohio," Weird U.S., http://www.weirdus.com/states/ohio/bizarre_beasts/bigfoot_cedar_bog/index.php.

Chapter 8

1. The Spalding Research Project, http://solomonspalding.com/SRP/saga2/sagawt0a.htm.
2. Ibid.
3. Ibid.
4. Giants of Ohio and the Mound Builders, http://www.burlingtonnews.net/ohiogiants.html.
5. Ibid.
6. Ibid.
7. Ibid.
8. The Cryptozoologist's Blog, http://www.myspace.com/the_cryptozoologist/blog/408331863.
9. Ibid.
10. Historical North American Giants, http://www.cavelore.com/giantus2.htm.
11. Ibid.
12. Ibid.

156

13. Ibid.
14. *Toledo Gazette*, January 28, 2010.
15. Ibid.
16. Eberhart, p. 403.
17. Clark, p. 250.
18. HSR.
19. Ibid.
20. Ibid.
21. Ibid.
22. Ibid.
23. Ibid.
24. Ibid.
25. Ibid.
26. Ibid.
27. Ibid.
28. Ibid.
29. Clark, p. 254.
30. Arment, *Varmints*, pp. 498-500.
31. Coghlan, *Dictionary*, p. 59.
32. *Bluffton News*, November 26, 1956.
33. Ron Schaffner email, June 26, 2002.
34. HSR.
35. Ibid.
36. Cryptozoology.com, http://www.cryptozoology.com/forum/topic_view_thread.php?tid=3&pid=360975.
37. Coghlan, *Further*, p. 77; "Nine-banded Armadillo," Wikipedia.
38. *Cleveland Plain Dealer*, April 19, 2007.
39. HSR.
40. Ibid.
41. Cryptomundo, http://www.cryptomundo.com/bigfoot-report/loveland-frog.
42. *Creature Chronicles*, No. 4, p. 5.
43. Ibid.
44. Cryptomundo, http://www.cryptomundo.com/bigfoot-report/loveland-frog.
45. "Loveland frog," Wikipedia.
46. Loveland Frog Festival, http://www.lovelandchamber.org/index.php?option=com_content&task=view&id=40&Itemid=195; The Loveland Frog Project, http://home.fuse.net/tswendel/LFP.htm.
47. The Loveland Frog Project.
48. Clark and Coleman, pp. 107-8.
49. Ibid., pp. 108-9.
50. Ibid., p. 109.
51. Godfrey, p. 195.
52. Ibid., p. 196-8.
53. *Delphos Herald*, November 1, 2006; Ohio DNR.
54. Coleman, pp. 165-6.
55. Ibid., p. 168.
56. Ibid.
57. *Cincinnati Enquirer*, August 18-19, 2004.
58. Coleman, pp. 184-5.
59. Ibid., pp. 185-6.
60. "Melon heads," Wikipedia.
61. Ibid.; Haunted Places and Urban Legends from Ohio, http://www.hauntedusa.org/melonhead.htm.
62. HSR.
63. Haunted Places and Urban Legends from Ohio.
64. HSR.
65. Ibid.
66. Ibid.
67. Ibid.
68. Ibid.
69. Ibid.
70. Ibid.
71. Ibid.
72. Ibid.
73. Ibid.
74. Ibid.
75. Ibid.
76. Ibid.

77. Ibid.
78. Ibid.
79. Ibid.
80. Ibid.
81. Ibid.
82. Ibid.
83. Ibid.
84. Ibid.
85. Ibid.
86. Ibid.
87. Ibid.
88. Ibid.
89. Ibid.
90. Ibid.
91. Ibid.
92. Ibid.

Selected

Bibliography

Books

Arment, Chad. "Black Panthers in North America." *North American Biofortean Review* Vol. 2, no. 1 (2000): 38-56.

—. *Boss Snakes*. Landisville, PA: Coachwhip Publications, 2008.

—. "Corals and Kings: Reports of an Unrecognized Snake in Ohio." *North American Biofortean Review* Vol. 2, no. 3 (December 2000): 44-46.

—. *The Historical Bigfoot*. Landisville, PA: Coachwhip Publications, 2006.

—. *Varmints*. Landisville, PA: Coachwhip Publications, 2010.

Arment, Chad, and Brad LaGrange. "Cougar in southern Ohio." *North American Biofortean Review* Vol. 2, no. 1 (2000): 8-9.

Bolgiano, Chris, and Jerry Roberts. *Eastern Cougar*. Mechanicsburg, PA: Stackpole Books, 2005.

Bord, Janet, and Colin Bord. *Alien Animals*. New York: HarperCollins, 1985.

—. *The Bigfoot Casebook*. Mechanicsburg, PA: Stackpole Books, 1982.

—. *Unexplained Mysteries of the 20th Century*. New York: McGraw-Hill, 1990.

Butz, Bob. *Beast of Never, Cat of God*. Guilford, CT: Lyons Press, 2005.

Clark, Jerome. *Unnatural Phenomena*. Santa Barbara, CA: ABC-CLIO, 2005.

Clark, Jerome, and Loren Coleman. *Creatures of the Outer Edge*. New York: Warner Books, 1978.

Coghlan, Ronan. *Cryptosup*. Bangor, No. Ireland: Xiphos Books, 2005.

—. *A Dictionary of Cryptozoology*. Bangor, No. Ireland: Xiphos Books, 2004.

—. *Further Cryptozoology*. Bangor, No. Ireland: Xiphos Books, 2007.

Coleman, Loren. *Mysterious America*. New York: Paraview Press, 2001.

Eberhart, George. *Mysterious Creatures*. Santa Barbara, CA: ABC-CLIO, 2002.

"From the Past: A Strange Ohio Beast." *North American Biofortean Review* Vol. 3, no. 2 (October 2001): 50.

Godfrey, Linda. *Hunting the American Werewolf*. Madison, WI: Trails Books, 2006.

Green, John. *Sasquatch: The Apes Among Us*. Blaine, WA: Hancock House, 1978.

Hall, Mark. *Thunderbirds*. New York: Paraview Press, 2004.

Herdendorf, Charles. "Investigation of the Lake Erie Monster." *North American Biofortean Review* Vol. 3, no. 1 (May 2001): 60-61.

Keel, John. *The Complete Guide to Mysterious Beings*. New York: Tor, 2002.

Kirk, John. *In the Domain of the Lake Monsters*. Bolton, Ontario: Key Porter Books, 1998.

Lutz, John, and Linda Lutz. "Century-Old Mystery Rises from the Shadows." *North American Biofortean Review* Vol. 3, no. 2 (October 2001): 30-50.

Murphy, Christopher. *Bigfoot Encounters in Ohio*. Blaine, WA: Hancock House, 2006.

Schaffner, Ron. "South Bay Bessie." *North American Biofortean Review* Vol. 1, no. 1 (April 1999): 35-40.

Shuker, Karl. *Mystery Cats of the World*. London: Robert Hale, 1989.

Sucik, Nick. "'Dinosaur' Sightings in the United States," in *Cryptozoology and the*

Investigation of Lesser-Known Mystery Animals, Chad Arment, ed. Landisville, PA: Coachwhip Publications, 2006

Internet Sources

Bigfoot Field Researchers Organization, http://www.bfro.net.
The Brown County Bigfoot Project, http://www.browncountybigfoot.com.
Central Ohio Bigfoot Research, http://blakemathys.com/sasquatch.html.
Creature Chronicles, http://blakemathys.com/creaturechronicles.html.
Cryptomundo, http://www.cryptomundo.com.
Gulf Coast Bigfoot Research Organization, http://gcbro.com.
Humanoid Sighting Reports, http://www.ufoinfo.com/humanoid/index.shtml.
Mark Turner's Mysterious World, http://markturnersmysteriousworld.blogspot. com.
Ohio Bigfoot Organization, http://ohiobigfootorganization.blogspot.com.
Ohio Mountain Lion Watch, http://ohiomountainlionwatch.wetpaint.com.
Ohio/Pennsylvania Bigfoot Research Group, http://sasquatchsearch.tripod.com.
Mad River Sasquatch Study Group, http://shadows-end0.tripod.com/MRSS. html.
Sasquatchpedia, http://www.squatchopedia.com/index.php/Main_Page.
TriState Bigfoot, http://www.tristatebigfoot.com.
USA Place Names Gazetteer, http://www.placenames.com/us.
Wikipedia, http://www.wikipedia.org.